GEMS
OF RABBI NACHMAN

BY
RABBI ARYEH KAPLAN

PUBLISHER'S PREFACE

In the Talmud (*Shabbos* 138b), the sages expressed fear that the Torah would be forgotten. Rabbi Shimon bar Yochai replied, "Heaven forbid that it will be forgotten!"

Commenting on this passage, Rabbi Nachman of Breslov said, "Many people are aware of this statement and therefore buy many books to assure that the Torah will not be forgotten. But if the books are not studied, the Torah will be forgotten anyway . . ."

This work contains many sayings from *Rabbi Nachman's Wisdom*, some of which are grouped under specific headings. In addition, it presents for the first time, a translation of some of his parables and tales, as well as a number of his most famous teachings from his major work, *Likutey Moharan*.

I wish to take this opportunity to express my thanks to Rabbi Aryeh Kaplan for his help in arranging the format, and to Mrs. Heny Wolkin, Mr. Zeleg Leader, and Mr. Shimon Ze'evi of Jerusalem, for their invaluable aid in the translation of the stories and parables.

DEDICATED TO THE MEMORY OF RABBI
ZVI ARYEH ROSENFELD WHO DEVOTED
HIS LIFE TO DISSEMINATING THE
TEACHINGS OF RABBI NACHMAN ZAL OF
BRESLOV
— *Kislev 11, 5739*

Rabbi Nachman is one of the best known and most often quoted of the Chassidic masters. A great-grandson of the Baal Shem Tov, he added an entirely new dimension to Chassidic teachings. Even after two centuries, his teachings have a meaningful message. Now, as before, he speaks to seeking generations.

To some, Rabbi Nachman is best known by his stories. These may be counted among the great classics of world literature, possessing profound depth that speaks to the very soul.

To others, Rabbi Nachman is the Great Kabbalist. His teachings shed light on some of the deepest mysteries, while at the same time enhancing them with meaning for the most average individual.

Still others know Rabbi Nachman through his main teachings. He stresses *Hisbodidus*—secluded prayer before G-d. He taught that one should never lose hope, and that good points are to be found in even the most debased individuals. His doctrine was one of joy, stressing that a man must find cause for happiness in everything that befalls him.

To his followers, however, Rabbi Nachman is more than all this. He is "the Rebbe"—the teacher, the guide, the master. His teachings are not the abstract thoughts of a past generation, but living words of inspiration and wisdom for life today.

This work is a translation of *Shevachay HaRan* and *Sichos HaRan,* a combined work that was first published several years after his passing. It contains his most often quoted teachings, its subjects ranging from simple everyday advice to the most esoteric Kabbalistic mysteries. It is where the Rebbe presents a way of life that has both depth and meaning.

Translating such a work into a modern idiom represented a major challenge, especially in view of its wide range of subject matter. One moves from the simple narratives of the mundane world to sublime poetry of the Kabbalistic mysteries, often within a single page. Of course this was Rabbi Nachman's strength. He could bring the man to the mystery, and the mystery to the man.

The Hebrew editions offered absolutely no clue as to the origin of the many Biblical, Talmudic, and Kabbalistic quotations found in the work. To trace all these has been one of the major tasks of the translator.

Our notes are intended to serve a dual purpose. First of all, they are to make this book intelligible to those with a limited background. All unfamiliar terms, personalities and events, are explained in detail. We also strove to provide additional insight for the serious student of Breslov. Since many of the Rebbe's teachings can best be understood in context with his related lessons, parallel sources are cited. The circumstances under which a particular lesson was revealed is also provided where the information is available. In a number of instances, we have been able to logically arrive at conclusions not recorded elsewhere.

We hope to be able to translate these notes into Hebrew and include them in a future edition of the original.

I would like to express my particular appreciation to Rabbi Zvi Aryeh (Leo) Rosenfeld for inspiring this project, meticulously editing the manuscript and comparing it with the original, and helping track down some of the more elusive sources.

I would also like to thank my good friends, Leibel Berger and Gedaliah Fleer for their suggestions and help.

Above all, my thanks go to my wife Tobie, for being a continuous source of inspiration and strength during the entire course of this project.

Spending these months immersed in Rabbi Nachman's works has been a source of inspiration that was, as Rabbi Nathan would say, "beyond the power of words to describe." It is my hope that they serve as a similar source of inspiration to those who read this book.

ARYEH KAPLAN

Rosh Chodesh Nissan, 5732

Herein is told
   an infintesimal portion
      of the awesome holiness of our Rebbe;
   may a Tzadik's memory be a blessing,
      his goodness, his piety,
      and his holy ways in serving G-d.

He is the Rebbe, the sainted Gaon,
   the holy Tzadik, foundation of the world,
      his eminence, our lord and master,
   the precious exalted lamp,
      the treasured concealed light —
   his glorious holy name is
      RABBI NACHMAN OF BRESLOV,
   may the memory of the holy Tzadik be a blessing;
      his praise is hushed —
   Author of the Likutey Moharan
      and other sacred works.

INTRODUCTION

I, Rabbi Nathan, son of Rabbi Naftali Hertz of Nemerov, fully realize than an account of our awesome holy Rebbe's life should be written.

I have therefore recorded a small portion of his saintly ways, from his earliest perception until his departure from this world in peace. I myself heard some of these accounts from the Rebbe's holy lips. Others were gleaned from those who knew him during his lifetime. Much of what is written here was seen with my own eyes.

The Rebbe had much opposition, and I know fully well that many will not believe these accounts. I will not let this deter me. Many people yearn for these words and have urged me to publish this volume.

Deep inside, my heart tells me that these words should be published for the sake of those who would follow them. It does not matter who initiated them—they are obviously pure and holy ways. How can I withhold this volume from those who sincerely thirst for it?

The truth is its own witness. Look at the Rebbe's writings with an unprejudiced eye and you yourself will see that he revealed concepts that cannot be perceived with the unaided human intellect. These teachings could only be attained from the highest source through holiness and purity.

It is impossible to go into further detail. Anything more would only be superfluous. As people say, "It is either unnecessary, or else it is futile."

At first my heart beat with uncertainty and I did not know which path to follow. Then I resolved that I would write freely, no matter what the consequences, "that future generations might know . . . and arise and tell it to their children."[1] They will see this book and walk in the footsteps marked along these paths.

It is self evident that these ways are precious and holy. Every man can follow them and bring himself close to G-d; for they apply to everyone, great and small alike.

No matter how low you are, you can follow the paths charted here. Have pity on your soul and consider your true purpose, and you will be worthy of eternal life, soaring like the Children of the Highest Abode.[2] Just be firm in your conviction, like a firmly driven stake that cannot be moved, never straying from the path mapped out in this book.

What we have recorded here is less than a drop in the ocean of the Rebbe's great holiness and outstanding quality. They tower high above, in a place where human intellect cannot penetrate.

We have no desire to retell any of the Rebbe's miracles and wonders. Our only concern is to present ideas that can bring others closer to G-d. Let them read this and learn a way.

Every one who saw our manuscripts praised them very highly. Their hearts were touched with a closeness to G-d and they urged me to publish them. They pre-

---

1. Ps. 78:6.
2. *Bnai Aliyah.* Cf. *Succah* 45b. *Sanhedrin* 97b.

vailed upon me with words [3] until I was bound to complete this task.

May G-d have mercy on us, and may we be worthy to walk in the ways of our fathers who served their Master with awe, until Zion and Jerusalem are rebuilt and all Israel shall fly like doves to their cotes. [4] May this be in our days, Amen.

3. Ezek. 53:13.
4. Isa. 60:5.

מים עמוקים דברי פי איש

The words of a man's mouth are as deep waters,

נחל נובע מקור חכמה

A FLOWING BROOK, A FOUNTAIN OF WISDOM.

Proverbs 18:4

THE LIFE OF RABBI NACHMAN

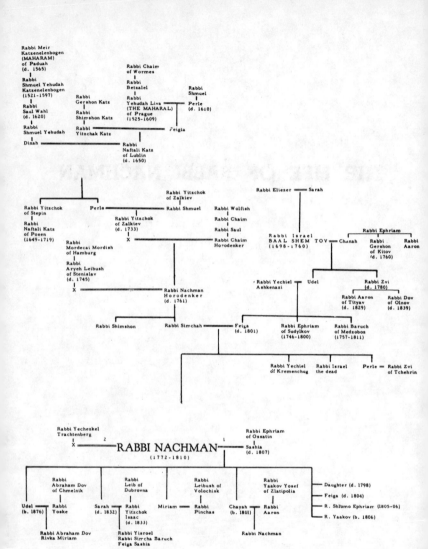

Rabbi Nachman's Family Tree

THE LIFE OF RABBI NACHMAN

Rabbi Nachman was born on a Sabbath, the first day of Nissan, 5532 (April 4, 1772), in Medzeboz, the town of his famed great-grandfather, the Baal Shem Tov. His father, Reb Simcha, was the son of Rabbi Nachman Horodenker,[1] a leading disciple of the Baal Shem Tov and a member of his household. Feiga, his mother, was the daughter of Udel, the Baal Shem Tov's only daughter, and she was said to be a divinely inspired Tzadekes. Rabbi Nachman had a brother Yechiel, who was later rabbi in Kremenchug, another brother, Yisroel the Dead,[2] and a sister Perle.[3] His two uncles, also sons of Udel, were Rabbi Ephraim of Sudlikov, auther of the *Degel Machneh Ephriam,* and Rabbi Baruch of Tulchin and later of Medzeboz.

Rabbi Nachman's birth occurred at a time when the Chassidic movement founded by the Baal Shem Tov was beginning to ebb. *Shabbos HaGodol,* the day he entered into the Covenant of Abraham, (April 11,

---

1. Rabbi Nachman Horodenker came from a very prominent lineage. For details regarding his ancestry, see *Nevey Tzadikim,* note on p. 9; *Margolis Tovah* (in Rabbi Avraham Zvi Margolis' *Keren Orah,* Jerusalem, 5724) p. 134; Rabbi Moshe Katz of Przemysl, *Megilas Yechusin,* in *Mateh Moshe,* Zolkiev 5505 (1745).

2. See *Shemos HaTzadikim.* He was so named because he was resurrected by the Baal Shem Tov, but not completely, and always had the visage of a dead man. The story is brought in detail in a manuscript recently mimeographed by the Jerusalem Breslover Chasidim. An older and somewhat different version appears in *Sefer Baal Shem Tov* (Jerusalem, 5722), introduction #75 (p. 31), quoting a letter from the "Rabbi of Medzeboz."

3. *Yemey Moharnat* p. 137b (#137).

1772), was the very day that the dire edict of *Cherem* was pronounced against the Chasidim.[4] Less than a half year later, Rabbi Dov Baer, the Maggid of Mezritch and spiritual heir of the Baal Shem Tov, was to pass away.

All of Rabbi Nachman's childhood was spent in Medzeboz. Shortly after his Bar Mitzvah at the age of thirteen, he was married to Sashia,[5] daughter of Rabbi Ephriam of Ossatin. He then moved in with his father-in-law in Ossatin, where he was to live for the next five years.

Even at this young age, Rabbi Nachman was already attracting a following. His first disciple, Reb Shimon ben Baer, attached himself to Rabbi Nachman shortly after his wedding, and remained his lifelong follower.

When Rabbi Nachman was about eighteen, his mother-in-law passed away. When his father-in-law remarried, the new mistress of the house made it very difficult for the young Tzadik to engage in usual devotions. He then moved to the nearby town of Medvedevka, where he was to live for ten years.

Supported by the Medvedevka community, the young Rebbe began to attract a substantial following. It was here that he was joined by Rabbi David of Tchehrin, who in turn attracted his friends, Rabbi Shmuel Isaac and Rabbi Yudel of Dashiv. Rabbi Yudel was a great Kabbalist in his own right, and was previously a disciple of Rabbi Pinchas of Koritz and of

4. See Nisan Mindel, *Rabbi Schneur Zalman* (Kehot, N. Y., 1971), p. 47; *Beth Rebbe*, chap. 4.

5. See *Alim LeTerufah* (Jerusalem, 5728), unnumbered letter written by Rabbi Nachman from Zaslav, dated Thursday, *P. Emor*, 5567 (6 Iyar).

his father-in-law, Rabbi Leib of Trastnitz. Rabbi Yudel and Rabbi Shmuel Isaac would travel 150 miles from Dashiv to Medvedevka to be with their Rebbe.[6]

Another important disciple attracted to the young Tzadik was the renowned Rabbi Yekusiel, Maggid of Terhovitza. One of the foremost disciples of Rabbi Dov Baer of Mezritch, he was a close associate of Rabbi Nachum of Tchernuble. Although advanced in years and a renowned Tzadik in his own right, he became an ardent follower and disciple of the young Rabbi Nachman.[7]

It was from Medvedevka that Rabbi Nachman set out on his pilgrimage to the Holy Land. On his return he stopped in Shpola to visit Rabbi Leib, the *Zeideh* or "Grandfather" of Shpola, who was later to become his chief antagonist. He also visited the renowned Rabbi Schneur Zalman, founder of *Chabad*, in an attempt to make peace between him and Rabbi Abraham Kalisker in the Holy Land.[8] After his return, Rabbi Nachman remained in Medvedevka for little over a year.

On the first day of Elul, 5560 (August 23, 1800), his oldest daughter Udel was married to Rabbi Yoske, son of Rabbi Avraham Dov of Chemelnik. Immediately after the wedding, he settled in Zlatipolia, where a crowd of over a hundred flocked to him on his first Rosh HaShanah there. The community invited him to bring his following to the large synagogue for the second day of Rosh HaShanah and Yom Kippur.

Rabbi Nachman did not approve of the cantor

---

6. *Kochavey Or* p. 24, *Nevey Tzadikim* p. 21.
7. *Kochavey Or* p. 29, *Nevey Tzadikim* p. 26.
8. *Avenehah Barzel* p. 34 (#46).

who was to lead the *Neilla* service that Yom Kippur.
When the cantor found himself unable to complete the
service, Rabbi Nachman made light of it. Enraged,
the cantor went to Shpola, a mere eighteen miles away,
and complained to Rabbi Leib. This triggered what
was to become a lifelong conflict on the part of the
Shpola Zeideh.

Despite the bitter conflict, Rabbi Nachman remained
in Zlatipolia for two years. During the summer of 5562
(1802), he was in Berditchov for a wedding and received
support from the sainted Rabbi Levi Yitzchok. After
consulting with his uncle, Rabbi Baruch, in Tulchin,
he reached the decision to relocate in Breslov.

On the way from Zlatipolia to Breslov, Rabbi
Nachman spent several days in Uman. Passing through
the old cemetery, where thousands of martyrs of the
Uman massacre are buried, he said that this would be
a choice location for his ultimate rest. He also came
in contact with the *Maskilim,* Chaikel Hurwitz[9] and
his two sons-in-law, Hersch Ber Hurwitz and Moshe
Landau.[10] They came to jeer, but were greatly impressed with his wisdom and invited him to remain
in Uman. These two events were later to have a great

---

9. *Kochavey Or, Sipurim Niflaim* p. 3. In *A History of Jewish
Literature* (4:476), Meyer Waxman writes, "In 1817, Heikel Hurwitz
(1750-1822) hailing from Uman . . . published a three volume work,
Zofnat Pa'aneah, which was a translation of a German book dealing
with the discovery of America."

10. *Kochavey Or, Ibid.* Moshe Landau is also mentioned in *Alim
LeTerufah,* unnumbered letter (after #172) dated Sunday, *P. Kedoshim,*
5595. Hurwitz and Landau, together with a Meir Horn, founded in
Uman one of the first secular Jewish schools in the Ukraine, some
time before 1822. See Jacob S. Raisin, *The Haskalah Movement in
Russia* (J.P.S., Philadelphia, 1913) p. 164.

effect in influencing Rabbi Nachman to spend his last months in Uman.

Rabbi Nachman arrived in Breslov on Tuesday, the 10th of Elul, 5562 (Sept. 3, 1802).[11] It was here that our detailed knowledge of Rabbi Nachman's life and teachings actually begins.

Breslov is situated just nine miles to the south of Nemerov, where there lived the Young Rabbi Nathan, son of a wealthy businessman, Reb Naftali Hertz. He was an outstanding scholar, seeking a true way to serve G-d. When a good friend, Reb Leib, described Rabbi Nachman's first Sabbath in Breslov, he decided that here he would find a mentor. Together with his close friend Reb Naftali, he set out for Breslov early Sunday morning.

Rabbi Nathan's first encounter with Rabbi Nachman took place on Sunday, the 22nd of Elul, 5562 (Sept. 18, 1802),[12] and it must be counted among the significant encounters in religious history. Rabbi Nachman was thirty years old, and at twenty-two, Rabbi Nathan was eight years his junior. Young as they both were, their meeting sparked a flame that still burns brightly.

Despite tremendous opposition from his family, Rabbi Nathan became a close follower of Rabbi Nachman. A week later he returned for Rosh HaShanah

11. The date is not recorded. It is merely brought that he came there at the beginning of Elul. *Tovos Zichronos* p. 7 (#5). We do, however, find that he arrived during the week of *Ki Tetze*. *Chayay Moharan* 28a (#12). The detail giving us the exact date is the fact that we are told that he arrived on Tuesday, the market day. *Avenehah Barzel* p. 8. (#6).

12. This date is also not recorded. However, we do find that he arrived on a Sunday. *Ibid.* p. 9. We also find that this was eight days before Rosh HaShanah. *Ibid.* p. 11.

and recorded his new master's lesson. At first, Rabbi
Nathan wrote these lessons down informally, but by
Chanukah he formalized these notes and began review-
ing them with Rabbi Nachman.

Rabbi Nathan was in Breslov again for the Sabbath
of Chanukah, and a third time on *Rosh Chodesh* Shevat.
He stayed with his master for the month between
Purim and Passover when the latter returned to Medvedevka for the wedding of his daughter Sarah. It was
around this time that Rabbi Nachman told his favorite
disciple to begin setting the main points of his teachings
in alphabetical order, forming the basis of the *Sefer
HaMidos.*

Rabbi Nachman said that his followers would
always be called Breslover Chasidim. He began his
custom of meeting with them six times a year to deliver a lesson. These meetings were held in Breslov on
Rosh HaShanah, on the Sabbath of Chanukah, and on
Shavuos. He would also visit his brother-in-law Rabbi
Zvi in Tchehrin, and Rabbi Yekusiel in Terhovitza,
where he spoke on *Shabbos Shirah, Shabbos Nachmu,*
and another unscheduled Sabbath in the winter.

During the summer of 5563 (1803), Rabbi Nachman met with some opposition on the part of his
uncle Rabbi Baruch, because of his alleged lack of
respect for the Baal Shem Tov. This opposition was
to last for almost five years. One of Rabbi Baruch's
disciples, Rabbi Moshe Tzvi of Savran, was to become
a great persecutor of the Breslover Chasidim after
the passing of both Rabbi Nachman and Rabbi Baruch.

In the beginning of Cheshvan 5565 (1804), Rabbi
Nachman's daughter Miriam was married to Rabbi
Pinchas, son of Rabbi Leibush of Volochisk. Rabbi
Nachman's first son, Shlomo Ephraim, was born

several months later, just before Rosh Chodesh Nissan. Between Passover and Shavuos, Rabbi Nachman took a mysterious journey to Sharograd, where he spent two weeks.[13]

It was also during this year that many of Rabbi Nachman's writings were systematized. Toward the beginning of the year he told Rabbi Nathan to arrange them in order and to copy the main points of each lesson. This was to form the basis of *Kitzur Lekutey Moharan,* an abridgement of his major work. Later that year, he told Rabbi Nathan to copy all his lessons in order.

With his close friend Rabbi Naftali dictating, Rabbi Nathan spent three months copying the diverse manuscripts, completing the task shortly before Shavuos. On Friday, the 17th of Sivan, 5565 (1805), this manuscript was given to be bound. On the same Friday, Rabbi Nachman revealed the secret of the Ten Psalms, discussed in the *Sichos* (#141). The manuscript was bound on the following Thursday. This was to become the first part of Rabbi Nachman's *magnum opus,* the *Lekutey Moharan.*

When the manuscript was completed, Rabbi Nachman told his disciple about another work that he was initiating. Completed early in 5566 and copied by Rabbi Nathan later that winter, this was later known as the *Burned Book (Sefer HaNisraf).* A short while later, a third work, later called the *Hidden Book (Sefer Ha-*

---

13. It is interesting to note that there is a tradition from the Baal Shem Tov that the inhabitants of Sharograd were decreed to be killed by fire and plague. *Shivechey HaBaal Shem Tov* (Jerusalem, 5729) p. 66, 68. Rabbi Nachman said that he was able to avert the plague. *Chayay Moharan* 29b (#18).

Ganuz), was also completed. Rabbi Nachman's followers knew of the existence of this third work, but it was
never revealed to them. Around Chanukah, the *Sefer
Hamidos* was also finally completed.

Early that summer, Rabbi Nachman sent Rabbi
Yudel and Rabbi Shmuel Isaac[14] to the surrounding
communities with the task of reading portions of the
Burned Book and distributing pages copied from the
manuscript of *Lekutey Moharan.*

Rabbi Nachman's fifteen month old son, Shlomo
Ephraim was suffering from tuberculosis, and he asked
these two messengers to pray for him. Despite their
prayers, however, Rabbi Nachman's young son passed
away shortly after Shavuos 5566 (1806).

Rabbi Nachman had great promise for his young
son and mourned him very deeply. He then spoke of
the "Master of the Field," whose task it is to correct
all souls.[15] He also spoke at length about the Messiah,
and Rabbi Nathan wrote the discussion in a *Hidden
Scroll (Megilas Sesarim)* in a cryptic abbreviated form.
Rabbi Nachman instructed that this never be revealed,
but a copy is known to exist among the Breslover
Chasidim. During this mournful summer, Rabbi Nachman began telling his tales, beginning with the story
of the Lost Princess.

On Yom Kippur 5567 (1806) a fire broke out in
Breslov during *Kol Nidre* service. Soldiers entered the
synagogue and beat the congregants because they would
not help fight the fire.

During Succos, Rabbi Nathan was forced to move
to Mohilev, sixty miles from Breslov. Because of the

---

14. *Nevey Tzadikim* p. 81.
15. *Lekutey Moharan* 65.

distance, his visits became restricted to the regular times of gathering.

Around Chanukah that year, Rabbi Nachman had another son, Yaakov. This child also died in his early childhood. As was his usual custom, Rabbi Nachman went to Tchehrin for *Shabbos Shirah* (7 Shevat). His daughter Sarah lived in nearby Kremenchug and he stayed there several weeks until she gave birth to a son, Israel. When Sarah suddenly became ill a few days after the child's circumcision, Rabbi Nachman hurried back to Breslov. He then began his fateful journey to Novoarch.

Like his journeys to Kamenetz and Sharograd, his flight to Novoarch was surrounded with mystery. Leaving a week before Purim, he spent the festival with the Rabbi of Novoarch, a distant relative. From there he travelled to Ostrog, where he summonded his wife, Sashia, who was dying from tuberculosis. She arrived in Ostrog for *Shabbos HaGadol* (10 Nissan), but was not satisfied with the medical facilities there and insisted on visiting the physicians in Saslov.

They arrived in Saslov on Sunday, just four days before the Passover. Despite the medical attention available there, Sashia passed away on the eve of Shavuos. From there, Rabbi Nachman travelled through Brody and Dubna, finally returning home to Breslov in the summer.

It was during this journey that Rabbi Nachman contracted tuberculosis. As soon as he began coughing, he predicted that this sickness would take his life. When asked the reason for the trip, he told the story of the Spider and the Fly.[16]

16. *Sipurey Maasios* 7.

During the Summer, he became engaged to his second wife, the daughter of Rabbi Yechezkel Trachtenberg of Brody. The wedding took place on the 15th of Elul, 5567 (Sept. 18, 1807).[17]

Two days after Yom Kippur 5568, Rabbi Nachman sent his attendant, Reb Michel, to Rabbi Nathan with instructions to bring his manuscript of *Lekutey Moharan*. He was instructed to write a table of contents for the manuscript and also to complete the *Burned Book*. Both these tasks were completed that day.

The day after Simchas Torah, Rabbi Nachman left for Lemberg (Lvov), where he sought treatment for his tuberculosis. It was at this time that he decided to publish the *Lekutey Moharan*. During Shevat and Teves (Jan. 1808) copies were sent to various leaders for approval for publication. Letters of approbation were secured from Rabbi Avraham Eliezer Horowitz, the Seer of Lublin (26 Teves); Rabbi Israel, the Maggid of Koznitz (4 Shevat); Rabbi Avraham Chaim of Zlatshiv (20 Shevat); Rabbi Meir of Brody (25 Shevat) and Rabbi Ephraim Zalman of Brody. Shortly before Purim, he sent Rabbi David of Tchehrin with instructions to have the *Lekutey Moharan* published in Ostrog. It was printed by Reb Shmuel ben Yesachar Baer Segal, and was completed shortly before Rosh HaShanah of the following year.

Reb Shimon had accompanied Rabbi Nachman to Lemberg, and shortly before Passover the Rebbe sent him back to Breslov with instructions to destroy both the original and Rabbi Nathan's copy of the *Burned*

17. *Alim LeTerufah,* unnumbered letter dated Tuesday, end of Av, 5567.

Book. After an eight month absence, Rabbi Nachman finally returned to Breslov on the 8th of Tammuz, 5568.

A month later, Rabbi Nathan also moved to Nemerov, where he could be near his master again after a near absence of two years. With the publication of the *Lekutey Moharan,* he immediately began working on a sequel, based on Rabbi Nachman's more recent lessons. This was to be the second part of *Lekutey Moharan,* and it was published shortly after the Rebbe's demise.

Shortly before Rosh Hashanah 5569, Rabbi Nachman distributed manuscripts of the second part of *Sefer HaMidos* to be copied by his followers. Around this time the *Shochet* of Teplik brought him a beautifully hand carved chair that had taken, six months to make. This is the chair that was smuggled piece by piece out of Russia and now stands in the Breslover Yeshiva in Jerusalem.

Rabbi Nachman spent the year 5569 quietly, recuperating from his illness. After Rosh HaShanah, he sent his brother Rabbi Yechiel, along with Rabbi Nathan and Reb Naftali, to pray for him at the grave of the Baal Shem Tov in Medzeboz. Although he continued to instruct his followers, he no longer travelled abroad. On *Shabbos Shirah* he fondly recalled how he used to travel to speak to his followers on that Sabbath.

In the summer of 5569 (1809), Rabbi Nachman's daughter Miriam left for the Holy Land, where her husband and father-in-law had settled four years earlier. Despite his infirmity, the Rebbe accompanied her on foot, saying, "One must walk with his own feet to the Land of Israel."

During the same summer, Rabbi Nathan was sent

to Berdichov to collect a debt from Rabbi Nachman's brother-in-law. Rabbi Levi Yitzchak, the saint of Berdichov, was then travelling through Walachia and Moldovia. It was at this time that Rabbi Nachman called Rabbi Levi Yitzchok the glory of our congregation, likening him to the Tefillin on the head of Israel.

Before Succos of 5570 (1809), it was impossible to obtain Esrogim until a day before the festival. The saintly Rabbi Levi Yitzchak passed away on the 25th of Tishrei (Oct. 5, 1809), and Rabbi Nachman alluded to this long before the news reached Breslov. During the ensuing winter, the Rebbe completed his storytelling with the tales of the Master of Prayer and the Seven Beggars.

Rabbi Nachman was then thinking of moving to Uman, and sent several of his followers from Teplik to investigate. His resolve to relocate was strengthened when his daughter Udel's child passed away on *Shabbos HaGadol*. There were also many fires in Breslov during Passover, but the Rebbe's house was untouched.

The fire was to reach Rabbi Nachman's house on *Rosh Chodesh* Iyar, 5570 (May 5, 1810). His house burned to the ground on that Friday evening, and he spent the night on a nearby mountain. He spent the remainder of the Sabbath in Reb Shimon's house. His belongings had been brought to the home of Reb Zelig, and he moved there after the Sabbath.

On this same Sunday, Rabbi Nachman received word from one of his Teplik followers that arrangements for him to move to Uman had been completed the previous week.

The Rebbe left Breslov on Tuesday morning, arriving in Uman on Thursday, the 5th of Iyar (May 9, 1810). Uman had been the scene of the great massacre of 1768 where thousands of Jews had been slaughtered by Gonta and his Haidmacks. Rabbi Nachman said that he now had the task of rectifying all these souls with his own death. It was also his desire to be buried in Uman's martyr-filled cemetery.

Upon his arrival in Uman, Rabbi Nachman moved into the home of a Reb Nachman Nathan, who had died the previous summer. He remained there until the day after Shavuos, when he moved in with Reb Yosef Shmuel. This house was cramped and did not have good ventilation, and right after Tisha B'Av the Rebbe moved into the house of a man from Lukatch, who had invited him to live there without charge. His new apartment was large and airy and had a good view overlooking a fragrant garden. It also had an excellent view of the old cemetery where the martyrs of the Uman massacre were buried. Rabbi Nachman praised this cemetery as the true beautiful garden.

Before Rosh HaShanah the Rebbe moved back to Reb Nachman Nathan's house, where the community would worship on the holy days. His condition began to deteriorate on Rosh HaShanah, and he coughed up large quantities of blood. Still, on the night of Rosh HaShanah he gave his usual lesson,[18] speaking at great length. This was to be the last time he would speak publicly.

His great weakness forced him to worship alone on the second day of Rosh HaShanah and again on Yom Kippur. Right after Yom Kippur, he dictated the remainder of his Rosh HaShanah lesson to Rabbi Nathan. This was to be his last lesson.

18. Brought in *Lekutey Moharan* B 8.

On the day after Yom Kippur, Rabbi Nachman asked to be moved back to the Lukatcher's house. He was very particular about the position of his bed, as if he were choosing the exact place from which he would leave this world. By Succos his condition had deteriorated to the point where he had to remain seated in a chair in order to be able to breath.

Rabbi Nachman's last day was the 18th of Tishrei, the fourth day of Succos. The final hours of his life are vividly described in Reb i Nathan's diary.[19]

We laid him on the bed, dressed in his fine silk robe. He told Reb Shimon to arrange his clothes and button his sleeves so that his shirt should not protrude from the robe. He mentioned to Reb Shimon to arrange it properly.

He then told us to wash the coughed up blood from his beard. We cleaned him, and he lay in bed feeling very free.

He took a small ball of wax and rolled it between his fingers, as he often did toward his last days when thinking deep thoughts. Even in this last hour his thoughts were flying through awesome worlds, and he rolled this ball of candlewax between his fingers with great lucidity of mind.

. . . . .

The house was filled with many people who had come to honor him. When they saw that the end was approaching, they began to say the prayers for Tzadikim in *Maaver Yabok*.[20]

We thought that he had already passed away and began crying, "Rebbe! Rebbe! To whom have you left us?"

He heard our voice and lifted his head, turning his awesome face to us as if to say, "I am not leaving you, heaven forbid!"

19. *Yemey Moharnat* p. 43.
20. "Crossing the Jabock," a collection of prayers and discourses on death, written by Rabbi Aaron Berachia of Modina (d. 1639).

It was not long before he passed away and was gathered to his fathers in great holiness and purity. Bright and clear, he passed away without any confusion whatsoever, without a single untoward gesture, in a state of awesome calmness.

Many people from the burial committee were there. They all said that they had seen many people die with clarity of thought, but they had never seen anything like this.

All this was what our meager understanding could perceive. But the true significance of his death cannot be comprehended at all. Whoever understands even a small amount of his greatness from his works, conversations and tales . . . will understand that it is utterly impossible to speak of such a wondrously unique passing from this world.

What should I say? How can I speak? What shall I return to G-d for being worthy of standing there when his soul departed? If I had come into the world for this alone it would be sufficient.

So, on the 18th day of Tishrei, 5571 (October 16, 1810), at the age of 38 years, six months, and eighteen days, Rabbi Nachman left this earthy abode. Each day of his life had brought a spark of divine light to all mankind.

Early the next day, he was laid to rest in the old cemetery in Uman. His grave is a shrine until this very day, visited by his followers from all over the world.

1   This is the way the Rebbe served G-d. All his devotion was concealed to such an extent that not a single person knew about it. He kept everything well hidden, cloaked in great secrecy.

At first, the Rebbe's way of serving G-d was one of extreme simplicity. He did not resort to any sophistication, but walked a very uncomplicated path.

When the Rebbe was involved in his devotions, everything he did required great toil and effort. No form of devotion came easily, and the Rebbe literally had to lay down his life in many cases. Each thing required tremendous effort, and he had to work hard each time he wanted to do something to serve G-d. He fell a thousand times, but each time he picked himself up again and served G-d anew.

The most difficult thing was to begin serving G-d and accept the yoke of true devotion. Each time he would begin, he would find himself falling. He would then begin anew and stumble yet another time. This occurred countless times, over and over again.

Finally the Rebbe resolved to stand fast and maintain his foothold without paying attention to anything else in the world. From then on, his heart was firm in its devotion to G-d. But even so, he went up and down very many times.

But by then he was determined that he would never abandon his devotion, no matter how many times he

2   The Rebbe devoted every available moment to his sacred studies. He spent much time studying the Talmud, the Codes, the Bible, the *Eyen Yaakov* [1] and the mystical books of the *Zohar* [2], the *Tikkuney*

1   "The Well of Jacob," a compilation of all the portions of the Talmud not dealing with legal questions.

2   The classic of Kabbalistic literature, written by Rabbi Shimon bar Yochai in the second century c.e.

Zohar [3], and the writings of the holy Ari [4]. He also delved into many other sacred works, especially those involving *Musar* [5].

The Rebbe said that his father's library contained all the small *Musar* books, and that he went through every one. He also spent much time with the *Reishis Chochmah* [16], stating that he reread this remarkable work countless times.

The Rebbe's unique expertise in all sacred literature was obvious. He was particularly unique in his knowledge of the Bible, the *Eyen Yaakov*, the Ari's writings, and the *Zohar* and *Tikkuney Zohar*, where literally no one could be compared to him.

He was fluent in the entire Torah. He could quote anything in the sacred literature as if the book was opened in front of him. It was like a table set before him, where he could see everything and choose what he desired. The entire scope of our sacred literature was like this, standing ready before his mind's eyes to be used whenever he desired. This can be seen to some extent in the Rebbe's writings.

3   The Rebbe engaged in very many fasts. Even while still in his teens he fasted from Sabbath to Sabbath many times. [18] There were occasions when he fasted from Sabbath to Sabbath twice in succession.

Although the Rebbe was a child of delights [19], raised in comfort, he was very thin. Still, he would disregard himself completely, fasting and mortifying

3   "Emendations of Zohar," a seventy chapter commentary on the first word of the Torah. Also written by Rabbi Shimon bar Yochai. See *Sichos* 285.

4   Rabbi Isaac Luria (1534-1572, dean of all Kabbalists and leader of the mystic community in Safed. ARI is an abbreviation of ha-*A*shkenazi *R*abbi *I*saac.

5   Books involving devotion and morality.

himself in every possible way. Once he fasted from Sabbath to Sabbath 18 times in a single year.

4   The main way the Rebbe attained what he did was simply through prayer and supplication before G-d. He was very consistent in this. He would beg and plead in every way possible, asking that G-d have mercy and make him worthy of true devotion and closeness.

The thing that helped him most was his prayers in the language he usually spoke, which was Yiddish. He would find a secluded place and set it aside to express his thoughts to G-d.

Speaking in his own language, he would beg and plead before G-d. He would make use of all sorts of arguments and logic, crying that it was fitting that G-d draw him close and help him in his devotion. He kept this up constantly, spending days and years engaged in such prayer.

His father's house had a small garret, partitioned off as a storehouse for hay and feed. Here young Rabbi Nachman would hide himself, chanting the Psalms and screaming quietly, begging G-d that he be worthy of drawing himself close to Him.

Besides this, the Rebbe made use of every published prayer he could find. He went through all the books of prayers available, and there was not a prayer that he did not repeat countless times. He recited them all, the Psalms, the *Shaarey Tzion*,[6] the prayers printed in the large Sidurim. He poured out his heart in every possible prayer and supplication, even those

---

6 . "The Gates of Zion," a book of devotional prayers compiled by the Kabbalist Rabbi Nathan Nateh Hanover and first published in Prague in 1662.

printed in Yiddish for women. Not a single one was omitted.

The Rebbe also had the custom of reciting all the supplications following each day's *Maamodos*.[7] He would say the prayers for all seven days of the week at one time.

He also had the practice of chanting only the verses in the Psalms speaking of prayer and the cry to G-d. He would go through the entire Book of Psalms in one stretch, saying only these verses and leaving out the rest.

But beyond all this, the main thing was his own prayers, emanating from his heart in his own language. He would pray and argue before G-d, making up petitions and arguments as he went along. He would beg and plead that G-d make him worthy of true devotion.

It was prayers such as these that helped the Rebbe achieve his greatness. We heard this explicitly from the Rebbe's own holy lips.

5 . When the Rebbe was speaking before G-d, petitions and supplications would pour forth from his heart, and he would often bring up some particularly good argument, or compose an especially fitting and well ordered prayer. He would take the prayers he particularly liked and preserve them in writing. These he would repeat many times.

These conversations with G-d were the Rebbe's most common practice. All his prayers had one single focus, that he should we worthy of drawing himself close to G-d. On many occasions he literally demanded this of G-d.

7 A compilation of readings from the Bible and Talmud for each day of the week. In his prayer book, Rabbi Yaakov Emden states that nothing is known of the origin of the *Maamados*.

6   Still, it always seemed to the Rebbe that all his prayers were being disregarded. He was sure that he was not wanted at all, and was being pushed further and further from any true devotion. For he saw the days and years passing, and he still felt far from G-d. After all his prayers, he felt that he had not been worthy of drawing close to G-d at all. It was as if his words were never heard, and he had been totally ignored all this time. It seemed as everything was being done to push him away from G-d.

But the Rebbe's resolve remained firm and he did not abandon his ground. It was not easy, for there were many things to discourage him. He prayed and pleaded before G-d, begging to be worthy of true devotion, and still he saw no results. He felt as if he was being totally ignored.

There were times when he became discouraged and let his conversations with G-d lapse for several days. But then he would remind himself that he should be ashamed for criticizing G-d's ways. He said to himself, "G-d is truly merciful and compassionate . . . He certainly wants to draw me near to him . . . "

He was then able to again strengthen his resolve. He would again begin anew, pleading and speaking before G-d.

7. No religious experience came easily for the Rebbe. Whenever he served G-d he experienced every possible hardship.

For example, he initially found it very difficult to sit alone in a special room for several hours, devoting himself to G-d. At first this was next to impossible for him. But instead of merely giving up, he forced himself, overcoming his basic nature by spending many hours meditating in his special room.

The same was true of his daily religious obligations. They burdened him like a heavy yoke, and he often felt that it would crush him. His difficulties were unimaginable.

But the Rebbe discovered a way that enabled him to bear even the heavy yoke of his devotion. Each day he would say to himeslf, "I only have this one day. I will ignore tomorrow and all future days. I only have this one day alone."

In this manner, the Rebbe was able to bear the yoke of his devotion for that day. It was only for one day, and for just a single day one can accept all sorts of burdens. It was only when one day's devotions were finished that the Rebbe accepted the next day's responsibilities.

This was the Rebbe's way. He would only consider one day at a time. In this manner, he was able to bear an extremely heavy yoke of devotion, a burden he could otherwise not endure at all.

For the Rebbe served G-d with all sorts of devotions requiring great exertion and effort. His routine was so difficult that it would have been absolutely impossible had he not considered each day as the only day.

8   The Rebbe's holy qualities were very apparent in his conquest of the universal desire, namely that of sex.

He told us that he had had countless temptations. Still, he insisted that sex was not really desirable and certainly not a difficult test to withstand.

The Rebbe said, "Any person, Jew or gentile alike, will not even think of sex as desirable if he is truly wise. If one knows anatomy and understands bodily functions, he should be absolutely repulsed by this desire." He spoke at length, but unfortunately most of the discussion was forgotten.

However, the general trend of his conversation was that the sexual act was ultimately repulsive. He emphasized this to such an extent that he once flatly said, "A man with even the smallest amount of true intelligence, will not find this a temptation at all." *

But there was a time in the Rebbe's youth when he had not yet subjugated this desire. At this time, he still had so many fearful sexual temptations that it is impossible to describe them in detail. In his youth, when his blood was literally burning, he had countless trials. He had many opportunities, and was in great danger time and again. But he was a stalwart warrior and overcame every evil desire. In this manner, he surmounted his temptations many times.

Despite this, the Rebbe did not seek to avoid such temptations. He actually wanted to be tested, and he prayed to G-d to set temptations before him. This is how much self confidence he had that he would not rebel against G-d. For he said, "How can one sin and disobey G-d, unless he is literally insane? But with just a little common sense all temptations can be overcome." So firmly was the Rebbe's heart resolved toward G-d. 8

With all this, the temptations were very real, and at the time, the Rebbe was in great peril. He would cry out to G-d, again and again, until he was able to surmount this evil.

Difficult as his trials were, the Rebbe still did not attempt to avoid them. Countless times he battled with his passions, until G-d helped him and he was able to subjugate his impulse completely.

8 *Shevachay Moharan* 3a (#3).

The Rebbe finally destroyed the fiery chamber of this universal desire completely. He then became very holy, totally separating himself from such pleasures. His separation was absolute, a great and awesome level of holiness.

The Rebbe said, "The forces of evil would concede me everything if I would only go along with this. I will concede to everything else, but this one thing I will surmount completely."

The Evil One was willing to let the Rebbe overcome every single desire, as long as the Rebbe conceded to one thing. In all probability this refers to sex, the most universal temptation. But the Rebbe said that he would do the opposite. He would ignore his other desires and not work to control them at all. But the sexual desire he would eradicate completely.

This is actually how the Rebbe began. At first he directed all his effort toward this one goal, to annihilate every vestige of sexual desire. He totally ignored such pleasures as eating, making no effort at all to subdue them. Indeed, he would eat very much, even more than most people. He said, "At that time, I was drawing all my desires into my appetite for food." But later, even this appetite was subdued. [9]

But do not think that such self control was a simple matter. In order to gain total control over his sexual instincts, the Rebbe had to battle countless temptations. It required many days and years of praying and begging and pouring out his heart before G-d, pleading that He rescue him from this desire.

The Rebbe continued along this path until he was able to withstand all temptation. He sanctified himself to such a degree that his total separation from this

[9]   *Chayay Moharan* 22a (#12).

desire cannot be imagined. In the end, he was worthy of totally subjugating it.

He worked on himself until he actually found it difficult to understand how people could consider this desire difficult to control. For to him it was no longer any temptation at all.

9 During his childhood, the Rebbe constantly visited the grave of the holy Baal Shem Tov. He would speak to his great-grandfather and ask him to help him draw close to G-d.

He would go at night, even during the great winter frosts. After leaving the gravesite, he would immerse in the Mikvah. [10]

The town of Medzebodz, where the Rebbe lived as a child, had two Mikvahs. One was inside the bathhouse, and the other in the outside courtyard. The Rebbe always chose to immerse in the outside Mikvah. This was even true during the great frosts, when he was thoroughly chilled from his trip to the Baal Shem Tov's grave.

It was a long walk from the Rebbe's house to the cemetery. Then the Rebbe could spend a long time at the grave. After this he had another long walk to the Mikvah. He would arrive there frozen, but would still use the outdoor Mikvah. He forced himself to do this in order to gain total self-mastery. All this took place late at night when he could not be seen.

I heard this from another, who heard it from the Rebbe's own holy lips. When he did this, the Rebbe was no more than six years old.

The Rebbe concealed his devotions to such an extent

10 A special ritual pool used for purification, prescribed in Lev. 11:32, cf. *Sifra ad loc., Yad Chazakah, Mikvaos* 1:2. He may have immersed upon returning from the cemetery because it is normally considered an unclean place.

that it often had humorous results. One icy winter morning he attended the Mikvah, and returned to the synagogue with dripping wet *Peyos* [11] The people looked at him with surprise, wondering why his hair was wet. They never imagined that such a young child was attending the Mikvah, and thought that he had washed his hair. But to wash one's hair early in the morning on such a frigid day seemed ludicrous, and they dismissed this as another one of his childish ways. No one ever imagined the truth, so completely did he conceal his devotions.

The same was true of his many great fasts. Not a single person knew about them, not even his parents and relatives. Only his wife knew that he was not taking his meals, and he made her swear not to reveal it. The Rebbe used every device possible to conceal his fasts, so that no one knew of them at all .

10   When the Rebbe left Medziboz and went to live with his father-in-law [12] there were still many occasions when he wanted to speak to the Baal Shem Tov. Since he could not actually visit his grave, he would go to the grave of the renowned Rabbi Yeshiah of Yanov in the nearby city of Smela [13]. He would ask

---

11   Long sidelocks grown in accordance to the Kabbalistic interpretation of Lev. 19:27. Cf. *Likutey Torah HaAri* and *Shaar HaMitzvòs ad loc.*

12   In Ossatin, where he lived between the ages of 13 and 18. See Chayay Moharan 25b (#2), 26a (#5),

13   Rabbi Yeshiah was a leading disciple of the Baal Shem Tov, and was the one to whom he entrusted his ethical will *Tzavaas HaBaal Shem Tov.* The traditional date ascribed to his death is 22 Iyar, 5534 (May 21, 1794), but this must be emended to an earlier date on the basis of what is written here. Rabbi Nachman left Ossatin around 1790.

the famed Tzadik to transmit his message to the Baal
Shem Tov, telling him what he needed[14].

11. The Rebbe spent most of his youth in the
village of Ossatin[15] near Medvedevka, where his father-
in-law lived.[16] This was near a large river [17] with many
reeds and rushes growing on its banks.

The Rebbe often took a small boat and by himself
rowed along the river. He could not control the boat
very well, but would still take it beyond the rushes
where he could not be seen. It was here that he secluded
himself in prayer before G-d. The Rebbe himself writes
that it was here that he attained what he did.

Although he could not control his boat very well,
the Rebbe often took it to the very middle of the river,
straying far from the shore. The boat would rock violent-
ly in the heavy current and seem ready to sink. The
Rebbe had no idea how to remedy the situation, and
would lift his hands and cry out to G-d with true
devotion.

The same thing happened later when he was in
Tiberias. Attempting to escape the plague, he found
himself on a narrow wall, hanging by his fingertips
above the Sea of Kineret. When he felt that he would
surely fall, he also cried out to G-d.

The Rebbe constantly repeated these stories. They

14. This was also carried out with great secrecy, see *Avenehah
Barzel, Sichos VeSipurim* #14.

15 Confused by many later writers with the city of Gusyatin
or Husyatin in the Western Ukraine. Ossatin was a small village near
Medvedevka and Smela, as we see here and above

16 Rabbi Nachman lived with his father-in-law, Reb Ephraim,
from the time he was married shortly after his thirteenth birthday,
until he was around eighteen. *Chayay Moharan* 25b (#2).

17 The Tiasman or Tyasman River, a tributary of the Dnieper.

were a lesson that he wanted to impress on our hearts and minds.

Imagine that you are in the middle of the sea, with a storm raging to the very heart of the heavens. You are hanging on by a hairbreadth, not knowing what to do. You do not even have time to cry out. You can only lift your eyes and heart to G-d.

You should always lift your heart to G-d like this. Seclude yourself and cry out to G-d. The danger is more than imaginary. As you know deep down in your soul, every man is in great danger in this world.

Understand these words well.

12. Whenever his high spiritual level was mentioned, the Rebbe would say, "But I worked very hard for all this. *Ich hab zehr gehoravet. Ich hab zehr fil gefast.* I struggled very much. I endured many fasts."

We are taught that "envy of scholars increases wisdom."[18] This is why the Rebbe told us all these things. He wanted us to envy his great achievements and emulate them, following his ways in striving to serve G-d.

The Rebbe once spoke to one of us about his attainments. He seemed to boast of his high level and deep perception just like one taunts another and tries to make him jealous of some mundane achievement.

The other replied to the Rebbe, "How can I achieve this? Who is worthy of attaining such a high level? Surely only one with a lofty soul like yours!"

The Rebbe seemed very irritated and answered, "This is the trouble. You think that Tzadikim attain greatness merely because they have a very great soul. This is absolutely wrong! Any person can attain my

18 . *Baba Basra* 21a.

levels and become just like me. All that it takes is true devotion and effort.'

13. The Rebbe also told us of his great shyness. He said, "I used to be so timid before G-d, I could literally feel the shame on my face. I would often stand before G-d and feel embarrassed, as if I had been humiliated in front of a friend. There were times when I would actually blush, so great was my shame."

This shame was always visible on the Rebbe's face. No one had ever seen anything like it before.

The great Tzadik, Rabbi Nachum of Tchernubal[19] once saw the Rebbe as a youth in Medvedevka. He was astounded at the great awe that was visible on the Rebbe's face. He said that on the Rebbe's face we can see the literal meaning of the verse (Ex. 20:17), "That His fear be on your faces, that you sin not."

14. The Rebbe's eyes would literally "glow like the sun and the moon."[20]

This was especially true on the holy Sabbath, when his eyes would shine and his face glow.

The Rebbe's great holiness and fiery bond with G-d on the Sabbath were really something to see. There was the way he said Kiddush on Friday evening and his customs at the table. There was the awesome melody with which he sang *Askinu Seudasa* and *Azamer BeShvachin.*[21] There was the way he sang the other

---

19   Rabbi Nachum was one of the disciples of the Baal Shem Tov. He died on 11 Cheshvan, 5558 (Oct. 31, 1797), shortly before the Rebbe left on his pilgrimage to Israel.

20   Saturday morning prayer, *Nishmas.*

21   "I Will Prepare the Meal," and "I Will Sing with Praises," both composed by the Ari.

Sabbath table songs, such as *Kol MeKadesh*, [22] *Menucha VeSimcha*, [23] *Eshes Chayil* [24] and *MeEyen Olom Habah*. [25] If you have not seen this, you have never seen anything good [26]

Those who were at the Rebbe's table on a Sabbath would be ready to bear witness that such a sight would never be seen again until the coming of the Messiah. If all the seas were ink,[570] it would still be impossible to describe even an inkling of the great beauty, the awesome sanctity, the deep awe, the pleasant comradeship, and the wonderful closeness to G-d that existed at the table. In true modesty, one could say that such a scene was never before witnessed.

I am only speaking of our own meager understanding of what was taking place there. Beyond that, there were deep mysteries far above our understanding.

Before Kiddush, the Rebbe would take the cup in his hand and stand in absolute silence for a long while. All we could hear was a faint yearning sound coming from his lips as he reached the lofty spheres whereto he ascended. Then, the Rebbe would begin the opening words of the Kiddush in a wondrous chant: "*Yom HaShishi* . . . The Sixth Day . . . "

[The Rebbe said, "The first word . . . "

---

22   "All Who Sanctify" (the Sabbath), most probably composed by Rabbi Moses ben Kalonymus of Mayence (10th century).

23   "Repose and Gladness," possibly by the same author.

24 . "A Woman of Valor," from Prov. 31:10-31. The order is interesting, because this is usually said before *Askinu Seudasa*.

25   "Like the World to Come," the last verse of *Mah Yedidus*, a Sabbath Table song probably composed by Rabbi Menachem ben Machir.

26   Cf. *Succos* 51a.

15   The Rebbe once gave his old Tallis to one of his esteemed followers.

He said, "Be very careful with this Tallis. I shed a tear for each thread in this Tallis until I understood the true meaning of a Tallis."

16   Before he passed away, the Rebbe said, "I have already reached such a level that I can no longer advance while still clothed in this earthly body.

"I yearn to put this body aside, for I cannot remain on one level."

Although the Rebbe attained the highest levels, he still strove to reach the next step. This was true throughout his life.   He finally reached so high a level, that he could no longer advance while still in a mortal body. He therefore had to leave this world.

He said, "I would like very much to remove this garment. For I cannot remain on one level. *Ich valt shoin gegeren das hemdel ois ge-tan. Varein ich kan oif ein medregah nit shtein.*"

17   The Rebbe displayed outstanding saintliness in overcoming his bad traits.

He told us a little of how he subdued his quick temper. At first he was very bad-tempered, becoming angry at the slightest provocation. But still, he wanted to be a good kind person, as G-d desires.

He began working on his temper until he overcame it completely. He rejected anger completely, pushing himself to the opposite extreme. In the place of anger, he now had absolute patience and tolerance.

The Rebbe thus reached a stage where nothing bothered him at all. He was so serene that nothing at all could annoy him. No matter how much bad a person did to him, he would tolerate it without any hatred what-soever. He would love his opponents, not bearing any ill feelings toward them at all.

The Rebbe was renowned for his outstanding serenity. There was a holy calmness about him, where nothing in the world could annoy or anger him. He was just absolutely good.

He became worthy of this in the Holy Land. In his works[27] the Rebbe revealed that only in the Holy Land can one attain true serenity, the opposite extreme of fierce anger. It was for this reason that Moses longed to cross over the Jordan to the Promised Land. We learn this from the verse (Ex. 34: 8), "And Moses hurried and bowed down to the ground." Our sages ask, "What did Moses see?" and answer that he saw great serenity [28].

The Rebbe also took pride in his great modesty. This may seem like a contradiction, but he was actually humble to the ultimate degree.

He said, "One has not attained true humility unless he is on such a high level that he himself can say that he is modest." This was the level of Moses, who could write about himself (Num. 12: 2), "And the man Moses was very humble, more so than any other man . . . " It was also the level of the saintly Rabbi Joseph, who said, "Do not mention that humility no longer exists, for I am still alive [29] '

The Rebbe also attained the level where he could take pride in his tremendous humility. For he had anni-hilated his ego completely.

---

27 *Lekutey Moharan* 155.
28 *Sanhedrin* 111b.
29 *Sotah* 49b. See *Lekutey Moharan* 4:7.

18   The Rebbe spoke out very strongly against those who thought that the main reason for a Tzadik's great attainments was the high level of his soul. He insisted that this was not true, maintaining that it depends completely on good deeds and effort. He was very specific in emphasizing this.

He said, "Every man can attain the highest level. It depends on nothing but your own free choice. You must truly care about yourself and carefully decide what good truly lies before you . . . For everything depends on a multitude of deeds ."

19   No matter how high he stood, the Rebbe was never satisfied with his accomplishments. He had involved himself in every type of devotion mentioned above, fasting and praying and forcing himself to do things to overcome his desires and emotions. He had already withstood every type of temptation, having spent days and years secluding himself with G-d, expressing his thoughts in his own words.

Constantly striving in this manner, he attained the highest spiritual levels. He had totally destroyed his ego, achieving a oneness with G-d on the level of the Children of the Highest Realm.

All this was attained while the Rebbe was literally in his childhood. He did not rest by day nor slumber by night. Never keeping still, he constantly devoted himself to G-d, day by day from his earliest childhood. And so, all this tremendous perception and awesome holiness were his while he was still a youth. He had already become one of the highest.

But even after this, he did not stop, never allowing himself to remain at one level. Every hour and every day, he would long and yearn for G-d, as if he had not done anything at all to serve Him.

The Rebbe was then in the Holy Land, and there attained a perception so high that it was beyond all measure. Still, from when he returned until the day he departed from the world, he always had this longing and yearning for G-d. He may have stood on the loftiest heights, but in his mind, he had not yet begun the climb.

It would consume many volumes to tell even the small amount we were worthy of understanding from what we saw with our own eyes and heard from his holy lips. For this was the Rebbe's way. He would constantly thirst for the G-dly, debasing himself with self pity, as if he had never inhaled the perfume of true devotion, and had not yet achieved even the level of a beginner.

To understand this, you must imagine a person who had committed every possible sin time and time again. Imagine now that such a person was aroused to true repentance. Try to depict the way he would look at himself. He would certainly have great humility and self-pity and be bitterly brokenhearted because of his past deeds. This is obvious and needs no lengthy explanation.

Consider the self-pity and broken heart of such a penitent. This would not be a thousandth, or even a millionth, of the great humility and self-pity and broken-heartedness that the Rebbe had each time before attaining a new degree of perception.

The Rebbe was a man who never rested or stood still. In the days of his greatness, he had already attained an awesome perception of the G-dly. Still he was not satisfied and continued to aspire. He accepted upon himself unparalleled suffering, abounding with prayers and petitions urging G-d to help him. He continued with a fearsome yearning, until he would finally attain a higher level of perception.

As soon as he achieved a new level, he would immediately begin anew. All his effort would be forgotten, as if he had not yet even taken the first step. He would then begin afresh, like one taking his first steps into the realm of holiness.

Often we heard the Rebbe say with longing and yearning, "How is one worthy of being a Jew?"[30] He would sincerely mean these words. for he truly felt that he had not yet really taken the first step. This occurred numerous times.

Although he reached awesomely high levels, he would constantly seek a higher level, ever soaring higher and higher. Still, he was never satisfied with himself. As soon as he reached a new level, he would again begin anew with a broken heart and deep humility, until he was able to attain a still higher step. This was always the Rebbe's way, even at the end.

Many times the Rebbe would say, "Now I know nothing, nothing, nothing at all." There were times when he would swear, "In truth, I know absolutely nothing at all[31]". This could even happen shortly after he had revealed words of enduring truth[32]. His wisdom shone forth, and still he insisted that he was totally ignorant. In this respect, the Rebbe was most unique.

The Rebbe said, "My teachings are very unique, but my ignorance is even more unique." That is, he

---

30   *Sichos* 159.
31   This occurred on *Shabbos Nachmu,* the Sabbath after Tisha B'av, 11 Av, 5570 (Aug. 11, 1810), in Uman, just about two months before his passing. See *Sichos* 153, *Yemey Moharnat* 35b, *Chayay Moharan* 43a (#31).
32   Cf. *Pesachim* 119a, *Baba Basra* 91b.

was unique in realizing his ultimate ignorance before G-d[33].

20 We heard from the Rebbe's own holy lips that some Tzadikim toil with devotion in order to reach a given level. They have a set level to which they aspire, and when they reach it they are satisfied. They are like servants of a king, who aspire to attain a particular rank of office through their efforts.

The Rebbe then said, "If I knew that I were now standing on the same level as yesterday, I would totally reject myself." He would consider remaining at yesterday's level the greatest detriment, for he constantly aspired to reach a higher step.

There is much to say here, but it cannot all be put into writing. Those who were worthy to see it with their own eyes, and hear it with their own ears, might be able to understand this to a small degree. They might perceive how the Rebbe never stood still at any level, but always yearned for the next step, until he was worthy . . . . This was always true of him.

Even according to our meager understanding, the Rebbe was unique in every way. Beyond this are marvelous wonders and hidden secrets. But suffice with this.

21 Therefore, even the fearsome wonders that we saw by the Rebbe are of no concern to us here. For according to his high level, these were not remarkable at all. Our only concern is to relate lessons of devotion, in order that an intelligent reader seeking the truth should be able to derive some inspiration.

33 *Yemey Moharnat, Sichos, loc. cit.*

There is no excuse in the world. Every person can aspire to the highest level, if only he follows the ways of the Rebbe recorded in this volume.

The main thing is prayer. Accustom yourself to beg and plead before G-d. Speak to Him in any language you understand—this is especially important. Beg Him to open your eyes. Ask Him to help you along the path of devotion. Plead that you be worthy of drawing close to Him.

The little we have written here should be enough for all who seek the truth.

THE WISDOM OF RABBI NACHMAN
Sichos HaRan

These are the holy whisperings on high,
　　the spirit of G-d speaking through him —
　　his word is on his tongue —
　　　　　to teach his disciples
　　who chose to approach him
　　　　to lead them along the path
　　up to the house of G-d
　　　　in piety and self-discipline.

THE WISDOM OF RABBI NACHMAN
Sichos HaRan

1. "For I know that G-d is great, our G-d above all others."

Psalms 135:5

These are King David's words; I know. I alone — for the vision of G-d's greatness cannot be shared.[1]

You may have a vision, but even with yourself you cannot share it. Today you may be inspired and see a new light. But tomorrow, you will no longer be able to communicate it, even to yourself. "I know." I—as I am now. For the vision cannot be brought back.

The Rebbe said: Look at the next verse, "All that G-d wants, He does, in heaven and on earth." It is a different thought, speaking of something else entirely, King David says, "I know," and can go no further, for words are no longer adequate.

A perception of G-d cannot be communicated. It is so lofty — higher than high,[2] that words cannot express it.

It is written (Prov. 31:23), "Her husband is known by the gates." The holy *Zohar*[3] states that the husband is the vision of G-d which each man perceives through

---

1. Cf. *Alim LeTerufah* 135.
2. Eccl. 5:7.
3. *Zohar* 1:103b.

You may fall to the lowest depths, heaven forbid. But no matter how far you have fallen, it is still forbidden to give up hope. Repentance is higher even than the Torah, and therefore, there is absolutely no place for despair.

If you are worthy, even your worst sins can be turned into something good. We are taught that sis can be transformed into virtue[8]. This idea may contain deep secrets but the main lesson is that one's failings and shortcomings can easily be returned to G-d. Nothing is beyond His power.

The most important thing is never to give up, but to continue to cry out and pray to G-d.[9]

3 The Rebbe said that all scientific discoveries and inventions come from on high. Without such inspiration, they could never be discovered. But when the time comes for an idea to be revealed to the world, the necessary inspiration is granted to a researcher from on high. A thought enters his mind, and it is thus revealed.[10]

Many people may have previously sought this idea, but it still eluded them. Only when the time comes for it to be revealed can the inspiration be found.

All inspiration comes from the place associated with the seeker. If one seeks secular wisdom, then it does not come from the Holy, but from the Other Side[11]

[The same is true when one discovers new meanings and ideas in his sacred studies. Were the ideas not granted from on high, it would never occur to him.

8   *Yoma* 56b.
9   Cf. *Sichos Moharan* 34a (#114).
10   *Kochavay Or*, p. 84, note 2.
11   *Sitra Achara*, a common Kabbalistic term for evil.

the gates of his own heart. The heart is hidden and the gates do not open to another[4].

2 The Rebbe emphasized G-d's greatness so much, it cannot be put into writing. He stressed that it is beyond all measure. G-d does so many wonderful things, that absolutely no one can realize them all. [5]

We may speak of G-d, but we know absolutely nothing. It is said that the goal of all knowledge of G-d is to realize that one is truly ignorant[6]. But even this cannot be attained.

This goal pertains to every facet of knowledge. One may reach the level of realizing his ignorance, but only in a particular area, and on a given level. There is still the next level, and this has not even been touched. He does not know enough about the next level even to realize his ignorance. And no matter how high he goes, there is still the next step.

A person therefore knows nothing, and still cannot perceive his ignorance. For there is always a level of ignorance on a step lying beyond his perception. [7]

The Rebbe also emphasized the high level of repentance.

<hr />

4. *Lekutey Halachos (Orech Chaim) Kerias Sh'ma 5, Alim LeTerufah 16, 160, 393, 423. See Sichos Moharan 34b* (#115), that this is the main perfection of faith.

5 *Chayay Moharan 16b (#8), Alim LeTerufah 15, 188, 227, 243, 276, 373, 413, 443, 444.*

6 *Chovos HaLevavos 1:10, beginning of Keser Shem Tov, Lekutey Moharan 24:8, Shevachay Moharan 8a (#42, 43), Parparos LeChochmah on Gittin 47a.*

7 This was said when Rabbi Nachman was moving from Breslov to Uman shortly before he passed away. *Chayay Moharan 16b (#8).* They were then riding in the coach and had met Reb M. of Teplik near Ladyzin. *Yemay Moharnat 34b, Chayay Moharan 38b (#1).* This occurred on Tuesday, 3 Iyar 5570 (May 7, 1810).

All wisdom comes from on high, each thing emanating from its proper place. Each idea has its own place, and there are thousands and thousands of different levels. All discoveries, sacred or profane, have a root above, each in its own particular place.]

4　The Evil Urge[12] is like a prankster running through a crowd showing his tightly closed hand. No one knows what he is holding. He goes up to each one and asks, "What do you suppose I have in my hand?"

Each one imagines that the closed hand contains just what he desires most. They all hurry and run after the prankster. Then, when he has tricked them all into following him, he opens his hand. It is completely empty.

The same is true of the Evil One. He fools the world, tricking it into following him. All men think that his hand contains what they desire. But in the end, he opens his hand. There is nothing in it and no desire is ever fulfilled.

Worldly pleasures are like sunbeams in a dark room. They may actually seem solid, but one who tries to grasp a sunbeam finds nothing in his hand. The same is true of all worldly desires.

5 .　Happy are we, for G-d has been good to us and given us the holiness of Judaism.

The Rebbe said, "I have great joy simply because I was worthy of being in the Land of Israel." [13]

12　*Yetzer HaRa,* the evil in man.

13　This and the statement below were said two months before the Rebbe's death, on Friday night, *Shabbas Nachmu,* 11 Av 5570 (Aug. 10, 1810). 　　*Chayay Moharan* 43a (#31), *Yemey Moharnat* 35b. The lesson given that night is in *Likutey Moharan* B 78.

The Rebbe's voyage to the Holy Land involved much confusion and many frustrations. Money for the trip was almost nonexistent. But still he overcame all barriers, and attained his goal of walking in the Holy Land.

He said, "I believe this and understand it fully well. The effort involved in every thought and movement when doing something holy is not wasted.

"When you want to do something holy, at first you are confused and unsure. You are standing on the balance deciding whether or not to do it, and barriers seem to be springing up on every side.

"Then you are worthy of completing the task. Your every movement, your every thought, and even the confusion you had in completing this deed, all are marked for good. They are lifted on high and made into very holy and exalted things."

Fortunate is one who is worthy of breaking down all barriers and completing each holy task.

6   When people want to become truly religious and serve G-d, they seem to be overwhelmed with confusion and frustrations. They find great barriers in their path and cannot decide what to do. The more they want to serve G-d, the more difficulty they encounter.

All the enthusiasm that such people have when trying to do good is very precious, even if their goal is not achieved. All their effort is counted like a sacrifice, in the category of (Ps. 44:23), "For Your sake, we are killed each day, we are counted like sheep for the slaughter." The *Tikuney Zohar* states that this verse speaks of both prayer and sacrifice.[14]

14   *Tikuney Zohar* 21 (59a). Cf. *Lekutey Moharan* B 46, *Sichos Moharan* 36a (#138), *Alim LeTerufah* 15.

When a person wants to pray, he encounters many distractions. But still, he gives himself over entirely to the task, exerting every effort to pray properly. Even if his prayer is not perfect, his very effort is like bringing a sacrifice, in the category of "For your sake we are killed each day."

The same is true of everything else in religion. You may wish to perfect yourself, but find yourself unable to do so completely. Still, the effort and suffering involved in the frustrated attempt are not in vain. They are all an offering to G-d, included in the verse. "For your sake we are killed each day, we are counted like sheep for the slaughter."

Therefore, always do your part, making every effort to serve G-d to the best of your ability. Whatever task lies in your hand, do it with all your might[15] Keep it up, even when all your efforts seem to be frustrated and all your attempts in vain. Do everything in your ability, and G-d will do what is good in His eyes[16]

7   The thoughts in one's mind are truly among G-d's wonders.

Thoughts exist in the mind in groupings, like bundles one on top of the other. When a person needs a fact, he remembers it by drawing it from its place in his mind. This itself is a great wonder, for where was this thought located until then?

There are many associations and symbols, all located in these parcels in the mind. One remembers a fact because he encounters some idea that stimulates the association and symbolism associated with a par-

---

15   Eccl. 9:10.
16   1 Sam. 3:18.

ticular thought. That idea is then brought forth out of all the parcels arranged in one's mind.

When a particular thought is withdrawn, then all the other thoughts in one's mind are turned over and rearranged in a different pattern. [It is just like the physical case, where removing something from a parcel or pile causes its entire order to be upset.]

8   Most people think of forgetting as a defect. But I consider it a great benefit.

If you did not forget, it would be utterly impossible to serve G-d. You would remember your entire past, and these memories would drag you down and not allow you to raise yourself to G-d. Whatever you did would be constantly disturbed by your memories of the past.

But G-d has given you the power to forget and disregard the past. The past is gone forever and never need be brought to mind. Because you can forget, you are no longer disturbed by the past.

This is very important to consider when serving G-d. Most people are distressed by past events, especially during prayer. When a person recites his prayers, his thoughts are constantly disturbed by memories of the past. He may think about his business or household affairs, worrying whether he did something wrong or neglected something important. While attempting to serve G-d through prayer or study, he might become troubled by his many sins and shortcomings. This is a universal problem, and each person knows his own difficulties.

The best advice for this is simply to forget. As soon as an event is over with, forget it completely and never think about it again. Understand this well, for it is a very important concept. [17]

9 People do not consider the ability to forget an advantage. But without it, it would be impossible to live in this world.

Imagine that you would constantly recall all that we know about the future world.

There is an angel with a thousand heads.

Each head has a thousand tongues.

Each tongue has a thousand voices.

Each voice has a thousand melodies.

Imagine the indescribable beauty of this angel's song.

If you could imagine such things without forgetting, you would constantly be comparing your own limited abilities to the immensity of such a being. It would be utterly impossible for you to endure life. You would be so disgusted with your worldly life, that you would die before your time.

If not for the power to forget, you would constantly recall your degraded state. You would constantly feel so disgustingly filthy with sin that you would be unable to lift yourself up to serve G-d. The power to forget is therefore a great benefit.

10 Do not be hurried. You may find many kinds of devotion in the sacred literature and ask, "When will I be able to fulfill even one of these devotions? How can I ever hope to keep them all?" Do not let this frustrate you.

Go slowly, step by step. Do not rush and try to grasp everything at once.

If you are overhasty and try to grasp everything

at once, you can become totally confused. When a house burns down, people often rescue the most worthless items. You can do the same in your confusion.

Proceed slowly, one step at a time. If you cannot do everything, it is not your fault. One under duress is exempted by G-d.[18]

Even though there are many things you cannot do, you should still yearn to fulfill them. The longing itself is a great thing, for G-d desires the heart.[19]

11   The Rebbe also said, "There will come a time when a simple religious man will be as rare and unique as the Baal Shem Tov."[20]

12 The world is a rotating wheel.

It is like a Dreidle, where everything goes in cycles. Man becomes angel, and angel becomes man. Head becomes foot, and foot becomes head. Everything goes in cycles, revolving and alternating. All things interchange, one from another and one to another, elevating the low and lowering the high[21]

All things have one root.

There are transcendental beings such as angels, which have no connection with the material.

There is the celestial world, whose essence is very tenuous.

Finally, there is the world below, which is completely physical.

---

18   Baba Kama 28b

19   *Sanhedrin* 106b

20   Cf. *Sichos Moharan* 25a (#11). This refers to one who even washes his hands before a meal. *Sichos VeSipurim* p. 76 (#6).

21   *Sh'mos Rabbah* 31:14. See *Shabbos* 151b, *Succah* 5:6, *Kesubos* 10:6.

All three come from different realms, but all have the same root.

All creation is like a rotating wheel, revolving and oscillating.

At one time something can be on top like a head with another on bottom like a foot.

Then the situation is reversed. Head becomes foot, and foot becomes head. Man becomes angel, and angel becomes man.

Our sages teach us that angels were cast down from heaven. They entered physical bodies and were subject to all worldly lusts [22]. Other angels were sent on missions to our world and had to clothe themselves in physical bodies.[23] We also find cases where human beings literally became angels [24].

For the world is like a rotating wheel. It spins like a Dreidle, with all things emanating from one root.

[The feet of some are also higher than the heads of others. For in the transcendental worlds, the lowest of an upper world is higher than the highest level of a lower one. And still, everything revolves in cycles.]

This is why we play with a Dreidle on Chanukah [25].
Chanukah is an aspect of the Holy Temple.

The primary concept of the Temple is the revolving wheel.

The Temple was in the category of "the superior below and the inferior above [26]." G-d lowered His pres-

---

22   *Targum J.* on Gen. 6:4, *Yalkut* 1:44.

23   *Targum J.* on Gen. 18:2.

24   *Targum J.* on Gen. 5:24, Num. 25:12. Cf. *Zohar Chadash* 20b, 21a.

25   Chanukah celebrates the defeat of the Greeks, the embodiment of Greek philosophy.

26   *Pesachim* 50a, *Baba Basra* 10b.

ence into the Temple and this is "the superior below."
The Temple's pattern was engraved on high, [27] "the
inferior above."

The Temple is therefore like a Dreidle, a rotating
wheel, where everything revolves and is reversed.

The Temple refutes philosophical logic.

G-d is above every transcendental concept, and it
is beyond all logic that He should constrict Himself
into the vessels of the Temple. "Behold the heaven, and
the heaven of heaven cannot contain You, how much less
this Temple [28]."

But G-d brought His presence into the Temple,
and so destroyed all philosophical logic.

Philosophy cannot explain how man can have any
influence on high. It cannot say how a mere animal can
be sacrificed and rise as a sweet savor [29] giving pleasure
to G-d. They explain that this pleasure is the fulfillment
of His will, but how can we even apply the concept of
desire to G-d?

But G-d placed His presence in the Temple and
accepts the animal as a sweet savor.

He made the fact contradict philosophical logic.

Such logic is crushed by the Dreidle, the rotating
wheel which brings the "superior below and the inferior
above."

Between potential and existence stands the power
of Hyle [30].

Before each thing exists in reality, it exists in

---

27 *Tanchuma, Pekudev* 1, *Zohar* 1:80b.
28 1 Ki. 8:27.
29 Gen. 8:21, Ex. 29:18, etc.
30 *Ramban* on Gen. 1:2, *Etz Chaim, Shaar Drushey ABYA* 1.

potential. Coming from potential to reality, it must first pass through the intermediate step of the Hyle.

All reality thus emerges from the Hyle.

The Hyle is therefore the source of all creation.

The three categories of creation—transcendental, celestial, physical—all come from this one root.

As they interchange, they all revolve around this root.

The letters on the Dreidle are *Heh, Nun, Gimel, Shin.*

Heh is *Hiyuli,* the Hyle.
Nun is *Nivdal,* the transcendental.
Gimel is *Galgal,* the celestial.
Shin is *Shafal,* the physical.

The Dreidle thus includes all creation.

It goes in cycles, alternating and revolving, one thing becoming another.

Chanukah means dedication. This is the dedication of the Holy Temple, "the superior below and the inferior above." This revolving wheel is the Dreidle.

Redemption is also an alternating cycle.

Like in the Temple, the superior are below and the inferior above.

When the Jews crossed the Red Sea after the redemption from Egypt, they sang (Ex. 15:17), "You brought them and planted them on the mount of Your inheritance . . . the Temple which Your hands established."

Redemption was for the sake of the Temple, the revolving wheel. For when the superior are below and the inferior above, it shows that all have one root.

This is the meaning of the letters on the Dreidle, *Gimel, Shin, Nun, Heh.* They are the first letters of the verse (Ps. 74:2), "You redeemed the tribe of Your inheritance, Mount Zion."

Gimel is *Go'alto*	— You redeemed
Shin is *Shevet*	— the tribe
Nun is *Nachalasecha*	— of Your inheritance
Heh is *Har Tzion*	— Mount Zion.

This is the category of "You brought them, You planted them on the Mount of Your inheritance." It is the aspect of the Holy Temple, symbolizing the revolving wheel which is the main concept of redemption.

This is discussed further in the lesson delivered on the same Chanukah, on the verses (Gen. 41:1), "And it came to pass at the end . . ." and (Isa. 49:10), "He with compassion will lead them." [31] This lesson speaks of the superior below and the inferior above, as well as the fact that Chanukah is the dedication of the Temple. The "surrounding powers" discussed in this lesson are an aspect of the Dreidle, the revolving wheel, since these surrounding powers encompass and rotate. [Wisdom here is the category of the Hyle.] Study the lesson carefully and you will understand.

After all this we can return to our original discussion. We have no need of philosophy, which is anyway strongly forbidden. We must have faith in G-d, that He created, sustains, and will eventually renew all worlds.

13   Guard your thoughts carefully, for thought can literally create a living thing.

The higher a faculty, the further it can reach.

You can kick something with your foot, but throw it higher with your hand. You can reach still further

---

31   *Lekutey Moharan* B 7. This lesson was also delivered on Shabbos Chanukah, 5570 (1809).

with your voice, calling to a person very far away.
Hearing reaches yet further, for you can hear sounds
like gunfire from a very great distance. Your sight
reaches even further, seeing things in the sky.

The higher the faculty, the further it can reach.
And highest of all is the mind, which can penetrate
the loftiest heights. You must therefore safeguard
your mind above all else.

14   The Rebbe often spoke about his childhood
piety. He said that he began anew many times each
day. He would begin the day with deep devotion, resolv-
ing that from then on he would be a true servant of G-d.
Then the temptation of a tasty meal or such would
get the better of him, and he would fall from his high
level of devotion. But on that same day he would begin
again, with new resolve toward true devotion.

The Rebbe would thus fall and begin anew several
times each day. He often told us how he continually
began serving G-d anew. [32]

This is an important rule in devotion.

Never let yourself fall completely.

There are many ways you can fall. At times your
prayer and devotion may seem utterly without meaning.
Strengthen yourself and begin anew. Act as if you
were just beginning to serve G-d. No matter how many
times you fall, rise up and start again. Do this again
and again, for otherwise you will never come close
to G-d.

Draw yourself toward G-d with all your might.

Remain strong, no matter how low you fall.

[32]   See *Shevechay* 6.

Whether you go up or down, always yearn to come close to G-d. You may be brought low, but cry out to G-d and do everything you can to serve Him in joy. For without this inner strength, you will never be able to truly approach G-d.

Keep pushing until you can do nothing else but serve G-d all your life. Be ready to do so even without a promise of reward.[33]

You may imagine that you are so far from G-d that you have no Future Reward. You must still serve Him as you can, even without such promise. It may seem that you are damned, but your responsibility is still there. Continue serving G-d as best you can. Snatch a good deed, a lesson, a prayer, and G-d will do what is good in his eyes.[34]

It is told that the Baal Shem Tov once became very dejected. He could find no inspiration and was sure he no longer merited the Future Reward. But then he said, "I love G-d — even without reward."

This is the only path to G-d, and no matter how lowly you are, you can still follow it. Strengthen yourself and begin anew, even many times each day. As time passes, you will then find yourself on the road leading to G-d. Amen.

15 It is not good to be old.[35]

There are pious and righteous elders, but to be old is not good. You must remain young, renewing yourself each day and making a fresh start.

Only one thing improves with age. The Talmud

---

33. *Avos* 1:3; *Alim LeTerufah* 264.
34. 1 Chr. 19:13.
35. *Alim LeTerufah* 210, 255, 276, 350. Cf. *Lekutey Moharan* 242.

teaches us that a pig becomes stronger as it grows older.[36]

16 Do not be a fanatic.

Serving G-d is not fanaticism. Those who pursue worldly goods are the true fanatics.

The world will consider you a lunatic if you abandon all worldliness in your quest for the G-dly. This is said to be fanaticism, and even this is not necessary. For you can serve G-d with restraint.[37]

17 Take my advice and do not let the world fool you. It may try to deceive you, but it will never let things end well for you.

Every man ends up badly in this world, even those who acquire all it has to offer. The harm is not only theirs, but also destroys many future generations. All the world knows this.

If the world is nothing, then what can you do?

To realize this, you must have help from on high.

But we need no further help, for the Torah has already taught us.[38]

The world says that you should not seek greatness. But I say that you should only seek greatness.

Seek out the greatest possible Tzadik. When you seek a Rabbi, choose only the greatest Tzadik.[39]

36   *Shabbos* 77b.
37   *Lekutey Halachos (Choshen Mishpat) Nichesay HaGer* 3:1.
38   *Ibid. (Even HaEzer) P'ru U'Revu* 3:34.
39   *Lekutey Moharan* 30:2.

The passions that destroy man do not really exist.

One must eat and drink but it is a necessity. The body must be sustained. One must likewise beget children. This is all necessity and not desire. It can be accomplished in holiness and purity.

Your mind can withstand any temptation.

It is written (Dan. 2:21), "G-d gives wisdom to the wise." Every man has the potential of wisdom. It is this potential that must be used.

This potential alone can overcome all temptations. But G-d also "gives wisdom to the wise," and this can grant you even greater strength.

You may have succumbed to desire and sinned in many ways. You may have blemished your intellect, making it confused and weak. But still you have some intelligence, and this alone can overcome all desires.

One grain of intelligence can overcome the world and all its temptations.

Wherever you are, you can be near to G-d.

You can approach G-d and truly serve Him even in the deepest pit of hell.

The Rebbe remarked that for this one needs tremendous effort or G-d's help. Sometimes one needs both.[179]

18   The best thing for children is to keep your distance from them, not playing with them too often. It is best not to pay attention to them at all.

The Talmud says, "Why do sages not have children who are equally learned? Because they do not begin with a blessing for the Torah." At that time, the Rebbe also mentioned an additional explanation.

When a child is conceived, his conception depends on the food previously eaten by his parents. They must sanctify and bless this "beginning," namely the things that precede conception, such as eating. Only when this is accomplished can a child be conceived in purity and holiness.

But there are sages "who do not *begin* with a blessing for the Torah." The "beginning" preceding conception, is not sanctified with the blessing of the Torah. For to have children who are sages, this "beginning" of conception must also be blessed with the Torah.

19   The world is full of strife.

There are wars between the great world powers.

There are conflicts within different localities.

There are feuds among families.

There is discord between neighbors.

There is friction within a household, between man and wife, between parents and children.

Life is short. People die every day. The day that has passed will never return, and death comes closer every day.

But people still fight and never once remember their goal in life.

All strife is identical.

The friction within a family is a counterpart of the wars between nations.

Each person in a household is the counterpart of a world power, and their quarrels are the wars between those powers.

The traits of each nation are also reflected in these individuals. Some nations are known for anger, others for blood-thirstiness. Each one has its particular trait.

The counterparts of these traits are found in each household.

You may wish to live in peace. You have no desire for strife. Still you are forced into dispute and conflict.

Nations are the same.

A nation may desire peace and make many concessions to achieve it. But no matter how much it tries to remain neutral, it can still be caught up in war. Two opposing sides can demand its allegiance until it is drawn into war against its will.

The same is true in a household.

Man is a miniature world. [40]

His essence contains the world and everything in it.

A man and his family contain the nations of the world, including all their battles.

A man living alone can become insane.

Within him are all the warring nations.

His personality is that of the victorious nation.

Each time a different nation is victorious, he must change completely, and this can drive him insane. He is alone and cannot express the war within him.

But when one lives with others, these battles are expressed toward his family and friends.

There may be strife in the household of a Tzadik. This too is a war between nations.

It is also the war between the twelve tribes, such as between Ephraim and Judah. [41]

---

40   *Zohar* 3:33b, *Tikuney Zohar* 69 (100b).
41   Isa. 11:13, Ezek. 37:16.

When the Messiah comes all wars will be abolished. [42]

The world will have eternal peace, as it is written (Isa. 11:9) "They will neither hurt nor destroy . . . "

20 Most things that people fear cannot harm them at all.

The only time a person can think clearly is when he is dead. When he is lying on the ground with his feet to the door [43] he will finally see the truth. For then he will realize that all his fear and apprehension was mere foolishness. All his concern was for nothing. For what can a mere mortal do to him?

The same is true of his desires and temptations. Lying there dead he will realize that he wasted his days in vain. [44] He will know that his most overwhelming desires were mere foolishness and silliness. For who really forced him?

But a person must die before he fully understands these things.

There is also a deeper meaning to this.

It is not the person who fears, but something else within him.

One may clearly realize that the thing he fears cannot harm him. Still he cannot help being terrified of it. This is because of that something within him which is responsible for his fear.

---

42   The Rebbe also once added that war will some day be abolished just like many foolish idolatrous practices once were. He also ridiculed the "wise men" who use their wisdom to invent weapons of destruction. *Sichos Moharan* 32b (#99).

43   Immediately after death, it is customary to place the corpse on the ground with his feet toward the door. *Derech Chaim*.

44   Cf. Ps. 78:33.

We actually see many people with ridiculous phobias. They themselves realize the foolishness of their fears, but they still cannot overcome them.

When we suddenly shout behind a person's back, he becomes startled. He exhibits fear even before he knows what is causing it. He can have fear without it entering his conscious mind.

But fear is not in the conscious mind, and therefore does not have to be rational. For the fear actually stems from something else within a person.

The same is true of desire.

One may realize that his desire is utter foolishness but it still remains strong.

Here again, it is not the person who desires, but something else within him.

Even when one realizes the foolishness of a desire, this something else continues to want it.

If you learn to understand yourself, you can rid yourself of all fears and desires. You must only realize that something else within you is responsible for them. Understand this and you can overcome everything.

You have free will.

You can easily train your mind to avoid the thing inside you that is responsible for your fears and desires.

21   Wedding Customs: [45]

45   These reasons were revealed to Rabbi Yudel and Rabbi Shmuel Isaac on Shemini Atzeres 5563 (Oct. 17, 1802), just a few weeks after the Rebbe arrived in Breslov. This was also just a few months before the wedding of his daughter Sarah. On the Sabbath after the wedding, 3 Nissan (Mar. 25, 1803), he delivered the lesson in *Lekutey Moharan* 49, also discussing these same customs. *Parparos LeChochmah a.l., Shevachey Moharan* 6a (#23).

It is customary that people get up and say humorous things by a wedding. It is also customary to begin by saying *"Ehla* — Rise!"

The Talmud says, "A woman may rise with her husband, but does not descend with him." [46]

People say "Rise!" along with the humor, for the bride will rise with her husband with every joy and pleasure, but not descend with him. [47]

It is customary to cover the bride's face with a veil. Rachel is "the beautiful girl who has no eyes." [48] This is the bride.

It is written (Prov. 25:2), "G-d's glory is to hide a thing." This also speaks of the bride. [49]

It is customary to throw baked goods at the groom.

It is written (Ezek. 1:20), "Wherever the spirit went . . . the *Ophanim* were lifted up.' [50]

An *Ophan* is an angel. Baked goods are *Ophin*. The similar spelling indicates a similarity in essence.

The spirit of the groom. [51]

Wherever the groom goes, baked goods are lifted up. [52]

---

46   *Kesubos* 48a, 61a.

47 .   A somewhat different reason is given in *Lekutey Moharan* 49:7.

48   *Zohar* 2:95a, *Netzutzey Oros* a.l., *Pri Etz Chaim, Kerias Sh'ma,* end of chap. 24. Rachel is the true bride of *Zer Anpin,* the transcendental groom. She has such pure faith that she is blind to anything that may question it. See *Lekutey Moharan* 62:5, above, 32.

49 .   "Glory" always refers to *Malchus* or Royalty, which in the Kaballah is personified by the transcendental bride Rachel.

50   The wording in the Hebrew text is somewhat different than the actual scripture.

51   Of the parts of the soul, *Ruach* or spirit is the counterpart of *Zer Anpin,* the groom. The *Ophanim* are angels of *Asiyah,* the lowest supernal world, which also corresponds to the feminine element. Throwing baked goods thus unites male and female.

52 .   See *Lekutey Halachos (Even HaEzer) Kiddushin* 2:8.

It is customary to give money to the dancers at a wedding. This is called "Sabbath Money."

It is written (Ps. 68:13), "Hosts of angels [53] throng and whirl, and she who stays home divides the spoil." [54]

The dancers "throng and whirl." When they are given money they "divide the spoil."

The revelation at Sinai was a wedding. It is written (Cant. 3:11), "His mother crowned him on the day of his wedding." This is the revelation at Sinai. [55]

Mount Sinai is also a ladder.

Take the letters of the word *SINaI* and turn them into numbers. The Gematriah then gives you *SuLaM—* ladder:

SINaI			SuLaM — Ladder		
Samech	=	60	*Samech*	=	60
Yud	=	10	*Lamed*	=	30
Nun	=	50	*Mem*	=	40
Yud	=	10			
					130
		130			

This is the ladder in Jacob's dream.

It is written (Gen. 28:12), "and behold a ladder . . . and angels of G-d went up and down on it."

The dancers go up and down, raising and lowering their bodies. They dance on the ladder of Sinai — the day of the wedding.

53 . The Biblical reading here is *Malchey*—kings. Here, however, the Talmudic reading of *Shabbos* 68b is used, namely *Malachey*—angels. A number of other places indicate that the verse actually speaks of angels, cf. *Mechilta* to Ex. 20:16, *Sh'mos Rabbah* 33:4, *Devarim Rabbah* 7:10, 11:3. This is resolved by a statement that the verse actually refers to the archangels, the "kings of angels." *BaMidbar Rabbah* 11:5, *Shir HaShirim Rabbah* 11:12, *Koheles Rabbah* 9:12; *Paneach Raza*, *Yisro*, p. 114b.

54 . See *Alim LeTerufah* 397.

55   *Taanis.* 4:8 (26b).

The money given to the dancers is called "Sabbath Money."

It is written, "She who stays home divides the spoil." This is the money given the dancers, as mentioned earlier.

In Hebrew, this verse is *U'Nevas Bayis T'chalek Shalel.* The first letters of the words spell out *ShaBaT* — the Sabbath. [56]

It is customary for the groom to give a scholarly discourse. It is written, "His mother crowned him on the day of his wedding." The wedding is the revelation at Sinai.

The groom speaks words of Torah, just as G-d did at Sinai.

It is customary to present the groom with gifts. These are called *Derashah Geshank* — "Discourse Gifts."

It is written (Ps. 68:19), "You have ascended on high, you have captured the prize, you have received gifts from among men." These are the gifts given to the groom.

It is said that the groom's lecture helps to unite the couple.

Before Jacob saw the dream of the ladder, it is written (Gen. 28:11), "And he lay down in that place."

"And he lay down" is *VaYiShKaB.* This also spells *VaYesh K B* — "and there are 22." These are the 22 letters of the Hebrew Alphabet. [57]

---

56   Cf. *Lekutey Moharan* 49:7.
57   *Tikuney Zohar* 18 (34a), 70 (132b), *Etz Chaim, Shaar HaYereach* 3; *Lekutey Moharan* B 79.

The lecture unites 22 letters into words of Torah, just like the couple is united.[58]

It is customary for the dancers to do *Pristakes,* raising and lowering their bodies.

It is written (Gen. 46:4), "I will go down to Egypt with you, and I will bring you up." This is symbolized by the up-and-down motions.

"I will go down with you to Egypt." The exile in Egypt was to gather together the holy sparks from Adam's wasted seed.[59]

"I will bring you up." When Israel left Egypt this was accomplished and the Covenant of Abraham was rectified.

A wedding is also a rectification of the Covenant.[60] We therefore dance to symbolize the exile and redemption.

It is customary to interrupt the bridegroom's lecture. This symbolizes the breaking of the Tablets.

It is customary for the best man to dress the bridegroom in the *Kittle,* a plain white linen robe.

It is written (*Ibid.*) "And Joseph will place his hand on your eyes." The son closes his father's eyes upon death.[61]

---

58 . Cant. 1:4 is interpreted to apply both to a happy marriage and to the 22 letters of the Torah in *Shir HaShirim Rabbah* 1:31, 32. Cf. *Etz Chaim loc. cit., Lekutey Moharan* B 89; *Kesubos* 10b.

59 . *Lekutey Moharan* B 5:10. Cf. *Shemonah Shaarim, Shaar Hamitzvos* on Deut. 16:3; *Shaar HaKavanos, Pesach* 1.

60 . This refers to the atonement of sexual sins, for a bridegroom is forgiven all his sins. *Yerushalmi, Bikurim* 3:3 (11b), *Rashi* on Gen. 36:3, *Magen Avraham* 573:0, *Bais Shmuel* 61:6. The giving of the Torah, the wedding of G-d and Israel, took place right after the Exodus.

61 . *Tur Yoreh Deah* 352. Cf. *Shabbos* 23:5 (151b).

Joseph is the best man. [62]

The *Kittel* is the garment of the dead. [63]

It is Joseph who makes this preparation for death.

It is customary for the dancers to do somersaults.

The revelation at Sinai was a wedding. There it is written (Ex. 19:3), "And Moses went up." It is also written (Ibid. 19:20), "And G-d descended onto Mount Sinai." Sinai then involved "the superior below and the inferior above." Thus the dancers engage in somersaults.

22   When a soul descends to this world, its destined task is elevated.

For example, when the soul of a scholar is born, scholarship in general is uplifted in the world. It will continue to rise from the day of his birth until the day he dies. Likewise, when a royal soul is born, military strategy and similar governmental concerns are enhanced.

The type of scholarship advanced by the soul will depend on the type of scholar into which the soul develops. The same is true of a royal soul. It can produce a benevolent kingdom or a wicked one.

In general, the task associated with a particular soul is uplifted from the day the soul enters the world.

In every man's life, there are years of strength, years of stability, and years of decline.

If a man lives seventy or eighty years, then the first third of his life will be his years of growth. The

---

62 . The best man makes the preparations for the groom just as Joseph paved the way for Jacob, who symbolizes the transcendental groom, as mentioned earlier. Cf. *Baba Basra* 123a.

63 . *Orech Chaim* 610:4 in *Hagah*. The groom wears the *kittel* to remind him that he too is mortal and therefore must repent.

next third will be those of stability, and the last third, those of decline.

For a third of your lifetime, you advance step by step along with all your powers and abilities. You then experience a phase where you stand still, and finally, the third of life when you are in your years of decline.

Your years of stability are those of fullness, when all your powers are perfect and complete.

You are then in the category of the opposition of the moon.

The new moon is very small.

Then it waxes until it opposes the sun [64] when it reaches its greatest size and remains stable. It then begins to wane and decrease in size.

Moisture is determined by the moon.

As the lunar cycle progresses, tides begin to rise higher. [65] Toward the end of this cycle, the moon wanes and the tides are reduced.

The more people repeat a statement, the more benign it becomes.

Often the Talmud says, "It is what people say.' [66]

There are non-Jewish sayings that enter Jewish conversation. These sayings are then elevated to become lofty concepts.

These sayings are like sea water.

It is too salty to drink. But when it travels through mountains of sand, it becomes fresh and sweet. For sand purifies water and makes it drinkable.

[64] . Cf. *Tosfos Yom Tov, Rosh HaShanah* 2:6, 8.

[65] . The highest tides during this cycle are called "spring tides," and occur during the periods of the new and full moon.

[66] . *Berachos* 2b, 5b, 48a, 62b; *Shabbos* 54a, 62b, 145b; *Yoma* 18a, 20b, 75b; *Taanis* 6b, 33a; *Megillah* 4a, 12a, 14b; *Chagigah* 2b, 15b; *Moed Katan* 9b, *Yebamos* 63b, *Gittin* 63b, *Baba Kama* 91a, 92b; *Baba Metzia* 59a, 85a; *Baba Basra* 5a, 16b; *Sanhedrin* 7a, 44a, 82a, 95b, 103a, etc.

The Rebbe did not elaborate this further.]

23 There is a light that shines in a thousand worlds [67]

This light is so intense that the average person cannot accept it.

It can only be accepted by a great sage who can divide the thousands into hundreds.

Such a sage can divide this great light into smaller portions that can be grasped by those below him. They can then receive it a little at a time.

A lesson may be so complex that it is incomprehensible. However, if it is broken into many simpler concepts, each one can be understood by itself. The entirᵉ lesson in this way becomes clear.

The same is true of the light that shines in a thousand worlds.

It is one simple light that cannot be perceived in part. A single concept, it can only be taken as a whole.

There is a scholar who is vengeful and vindictive like a snake. He can divide the thousands into hundreds.

Such a sage can divide this great light into portions that can be comprehended and accepted.

It is written (Prov. 17:9), "He who harps on something, separates a prince."

Rashi writes that "he who harps," is one who is

---

67 This was said before Chanukah 5567 (1806), during the week of the circumcision of the Rebbe's son Yaakov. *Chayay Moharan* 15b. It was said on the "watch night," the night before his son's circumcision. *Avanehah Barzel* p. 32 (#41). The child was born on a Sabbath, and this lesson was delivered when Reb L. Dayin brought the Rebbe fish for the circumcision feast. *Yemey Moharnat* 14a. For a detailed explanation of this lesson, see *Lekutey Halachos* (*Choshen Mishpat*) *Edus* 4, (*Orech Chaim*) *Pesach* 9, (*Even AaEezer*) *Kiddushin* 3:16; *Zimras HaAretz* p. 105b.

vengeful and vindictive, harping on what another does
to him.

Through this, he "separates a prince" — he separates himself from G-d, who is the L-rd and Prince of
the universe.

This refers to an ordinary individual. A sage, however, has a duty to be vengeful and vindictive.

The Talmud teaches us, "Every sage who is not
vengeful and vindictive like a snake, is no scholar." [68]

This verse also speaks of the vengeful and vindictive sage who can divide the thousands into hundreds.

"He who harps on something" and is vengeful
and vindictive, "separates the Prince."

A prince is an *ALuF*, a leader of thousands. *AeLeF*
is a thousand.

"He who harps on something" — the vengeful
and vindictive sage — "separates the thousands" —
and divides the thousands into hundreds.

The Talmud teaches us, "If you see a sage who
is vengeful and vindictive like a snake, bind him around
your waist." [69] Rashi explains that "you will eventually
derive benefit from his scholarship."

Such a vindictive sage can divide the great light
into portions, separating the thousands into hundreds.

Therefore, "you will eventually benefit from his
scholarship." For without him, the light is so great
that you will not be able to grasp it.

There is a logical reason why only a vengeful sage

68   *Yoma* 22b.
69   *Shabbos* 63a.

can divide thousands into hundreds, but it is very deep indeed.

One who understands it can bring the dead back to life. He is the one spoken of when the Talmud teaches us, "a time will come when Tzadikim will resurrect the dead."

One who understands this, truly understands death.

When one divides the thousands into hundreds, he brings the thousand into the hundred and makes death into hundreds.

Thousand is *Aelef* — the letter *Aleph*.

Death is *MaWeS* — *Mem Vav Tav*.

Bring the thousands into death — bring the *Aleph* into *MaWeS*, and you have *Mem Aleph Vav Tav* — *MAyoWS* — the hundreds.

Bring the thousands into death and you have the hundreds.

24 The Talmud teaches us, "In the future, G-d will grant 310 worlds to each Tzadik' [70]

Consider a single world. Think how many houses and courtyards and streets and cities and nations it contains.

Imagine the immense size of a single world. Consider the infinite number of awesome and wonderful stars, planets and galaxies it contains.

This is just a single world. Then try to imagine the 310 worlds that will be granted to each Tzadik. Think of the greatness and immeasurable delight that they will contain.

Each Tzadik builds his 310 worlds through conflict. Every word of strife is a stone.

---

70 .   End of *Uktzin*. This is explained in detail in *Lekutey Halackos* (*Yoreh Deah*) *Mezuzah* 4; *Zimras HaAretz* 106b.

The letters of the words are called stones. Thus the *Sefer HaYetzirah*[71] states, "two stones build two houses . . . "[72]

Words of strife are built of slippery stones.[73]

Strife is *maChLoKes*. Slippery is *meChuLaKim*. Stones created through strife are therefore slippery and cannot be joined.

A Tzadik can join these slippery stones.

He can then build them into houses.

He makes peace between these stones, arranging them and joining them together until a house is built.

This is the peaceful home.[74]

The Tzadik builds a peaceful home out of these slippery conflicting stones.

Out of these houses he then builds a city, then a universe, until all 310 worlds are completed.

It is written (Prov. 8:21), "That I may give those who love Me substance."

"Substance" is *YeSh — Yud Shin*, adding up to 310. These are the 310 worlds.[75]

"That I may give those who love me 310."

[This is spelled out as a reward for love. Love and peace are what cement the slippery stones so that they might build the 310 worlds.]

After his dispute with Naval, Abigail told King

71   "The Book of Creation," the earliest Kabbalistic work, traditionally attributed to the patriarch Abraham, see *Shem HaGedolim, Sefarim, Samech* 54.

72   *Sefer HaYetzirah* 4:12. Cf. *Lekutey Moharan* 18:6, B 8:6, 79.

73   Cf. 1 Sam. 17:40, *Zohar* 3:272a.

74   Cf. *Shabbos* 23b, *Lekutey Moharan* 14:10.

75   This is actually the derivation in *Uktzin, loc. cit.*

David, "Now I know that G-d will make you a house." [76]

This dispute will provide the stones for G-d to make you a house.

A Tzadik inclines to the side of kindness. [77]

He even presumes the merit of those who oppose him. [78]

The world cannot endure the light of a Tzadik.

Those who oppose the Tzadik obscure his light enough so that the world can bear it.

A truly great Tzadik must also face many judgements and accusations on high. [79]

Those who oppose him silence these judgements and accusations.

A man is on trial for a serious offense.

Suddenly another person becomes filled with zeal and says, "I will judge him myself and take vengeance on him."

The others who wanted to bring the defendant to judgement are then silenced.

There are times when the defendant would find it impossible to endure the judgement of his original adversaries. The one who wishes to take personal vengeance is then actually doing him a favor.

It is better for him to endure the judgement of the individual than that of the many. He can bear the former, but the latter would be too much for him.

---

76   These are áctually closer to Nathan's words to David in 2 Sam. 7:11. Abigail's words are in 1 Sam. 25:28.

77   Cf. *Rosh HaShanah* 17a.

78   *Avos* 1:6, *Shavuos* 30a, *Lekutey Moharan* 282.

79   *Yebamos* 122b.

It is written (Num. 25:11), "Pinchas . . . turned My wrath away from the children of Israel, when he took my revenge among them, and I did not destroy them."

Pinchas killed the sinner Zimri, taking the judgement into his own hands.[80] Had he not done this, the Jewish people would have been sentenced to annihilation. But because Pinchas took G-d's vengeance into his own hands, the accusation against the Jews was silenced.

This is the meaning of the above verse.

A man stands up against a Tzadik. He says, "I will act against him! I will show him my strength and revenge!"

This man is actually silencing all other judgements against the Tzadik.

There is another benefit that comes from such conflict.

Before a Tzadik can rise from one level to the next, he is first tested.[81]

Those who can advance are called (Dan. 1:4), "those who have the power to stand in the King's palace."[353]

The King's Palace is the mouth of a Tzadik.

Palace is *HaYChaL*. Turn the letters into numbers and the Gematria gives you G-d's name *AD-NoY*:[82]

80   Num. 25:8.
81   Cf. *Sh'mos Rabbah* 2:3.
82   *Tikuney Zohar* 18 (32a, 33b); Lekutey Moharan 55:7.

HaYChaL — Palace		AD-NoY	
Heh	= 5	Aleph	= 1
Yud	= 10	Dalet	= 4
Kaf	= 20	Nun	= 50
Lamed	= 30	Yud	= 10
	65		65

The Name *AD-NoY* is associated with *Malchus,* the divine attribute of Royalty.[355]

Royalty is the mouth of the transcendental form, as we are taught, "Royalty is the mouth."[356]

The King's Palace is therefore the mouth of a Tzadik.

When one Tzadik opposes another, it is a test to see if the latter can stand in the King's Palace. One Tzadik is tested to determine if he can withstand the mouth of his counterpart.

When he withstands this test he is elevated to the next level. The dispute is therefore for his benefit.

25. A religious discussion creates both Direct Light and Reflected light.

When you speak to a friend about G-dliness, the information he receives from you is Direct Light. What you gain from him is Reflected Light.

Sometimes the Reflected Light precedes the Direct Light.

Your friend may have a weak intellect and not be able to grasp your words. You, however, are still able to gain from the conversation.

Since you gain somthing from your friend before he obtains anything from you, the Reflected Light precedes the Direct Light.

26   It is written (Prov. 19:3), "A man's own folly perverts his way, and he casts his grudge upon G-d."

This speaks of one who does not bind himself to a true Tzadik. Such a person may appear to serve G-d, but all his devotion is like the contortions one uses when trying to mimic another. He is like an ape trying to mimic a man.[391]

"A man's own folly perverts his way." Because of his folly, all his devotion "perverts his way." He perverts and contorts himself, aping an ideal he cannot grasp.

The reason is because "he casts his grudge upon G-d."

27   The Rebbe once spoke about those who are religious for a while and then fall away. He said that even the short time that they are religious is very dear to G-d, no matter what happens later.

It is written (Cant. 4:9), "You have heartened Me with one of your eyes." G-d is speaking to the Jewish people, recalling the time they accepted the Torah.

The Midrash asks why the verse says "with *one* of your eyes." It answers that the other eye was already looking at the Golden Calf.

Even when they accepted the Torah, they already had plans to stray. Still, the short time they were close to G-d was still very dear to Him. He therefore said, "you have heartened Me with one of your eyes."

28.   Sexual temptations result from depression. You should therefore make every effort always to be joyful.

The Rebbe said, "Even when one is trapped in quicksand, he screams and screams and screams. *Un*

*afilu as me-falt in a blutte arein, shreit men, un meh
shreit, un meh shreit.''*   The Rebbe then raised his
hands slightly and said no more.

The Rebbe then spoke about the disturbing thoughts
that often trouble a person in this area. He quoted the
Talmudical maxim, "Trouble is bad enough when it
comes," adding "One should not be disturbed by this
either before or afterward."

29⌋ Lesson 275 in *Lekutey Moharan* begins with
the statement, "Every good deed that one does is made
into a lamp."

One of my companions told me that the Rebbe
once explained this idea in greater detail:

Some people have a light that burns only for a
short time. While it burns they can explore the King's
storehouse.[83] But then it burns out and they can no
longer seek.

Another may have a lamp that burns longer.
He has more time to probe the celestial treasuries.
Still another may have a lamp that blazes for an
entire day or even longer.

But there is one who has the most wonderful lamps
of all. These are never extinguished but burn and shine
forever. The owner of these lamps can delve into the
King's treasuries for as long as he wishes.

From this we can understand that even an ordinary
religious man can explore the King's treasury, but
only for a given time as determined by his good deeds.
Even this is certainly a most wonderful privilege. You
can find wonderful treasures even in this short time
and then enjoy them in the Future World forever.

[83] This understanding is the primary reward in the Future Life,
Cf. *Zohar* 2:166b.

All of your future life is determined by what you find during the time of exploration. If you are worthy of more time in which the lamps created by your deeds shine, you will certainly find more good in the King's treasury. It all depends how long your lamp can burn.

The light of a great Tzadik is never extinguished. His exploration of the King's treasuries can go on forever.

30 Once there were two close friends who had recently been married. The first one saw the other doing something improper, straying from the true path. However, he did not pay any attention to it, thinking it to be a mere accident. But when he saw his friend continue and do something much worse, he realized that the other was actually a sinner. He decided that he would have nothing to do with his old friend and estranged himself from him completely.

All this time, they had been supported by their fathers-in-law, as was the custom. After a while, they left their in-law's table and had to earn their own living.

The sinner began to prosper and eventually grow very rich. His friend, on the other hand, became very poor, and was constantly upset, complaining of G-d's injustice. He said to himself, "I know that my former companion commited a great sin. Why is he given such greatness and wealth?"

One evening the poor man had a vision. He saw a band of men approach, carrying large sacks of coins. As they approached, he could hear the loud clinking sound.

He tried to move toward them, but they stopped him with a warning. "Do not touch any of this money. It all belongs to your former friend."

Realizing that this was an opportune moment, he asked them, "Why is he worthy of this riches? I myself saw him commit a great sin!"

They answered, "From the day you both left your father-in-laws' table, your companion has consistently set aside times for Torah. He has taken upon himself to study a given amount each day without fail. But you are not involved in the Torah. Consequently, your companion is worthy of riches despite his great sin. For though it can extinguish good deeds, sin cannot extinguish Torah."[84]

"Sin cannot extinguish Torah" in Hebrew, is *We'ain Averah Mekabeh Torah*. The first letters of these words spell *MAoWT* — money.

31. The Rebbe's lesson on the verse (Ex. 6:9), "And they hearkened not to Moses because of impatience of spirit and cruel bondage," appears in the second part of *Lekutey Moharan* #86. The lesson states that the fact that one must work hard toward something implies a lack of faith.[85]

When the Rebbe addressed this lesson to me I was quite shocked. I always thought of myself as having faith, and could not understand his implication.

When I mentioned this to the Rebbe he answered me with some impatience, "You may have faith, but you have no faith in yourself. *Hast-di in dir kein Emunah nit.*"

84   *Sotah* 21a.
85   This lesson was given shortly before Rosh Hashanah 5558. *Parparos LeChochma* 61:8. Rabbi Nathan had arrived in Breslov on Saturday night for Selichos and spoken to the Rebbe after the service. A week later on Rosh HaShanah, the lesson "Rabbi Shimon Rejoiced," mentioned below, was revealed. *Yemey Moharnat* 20b, *Chayay Moharan* 15a.

The Rebbe told me this:

It is written (Zech. 4:10), "Who has *despised* **the** day of *small* things." The Talmud comments on **this** saying, "Why are the tables of the Tzadikim *despised* in the Future World? Because of their own *smallness*." That is, because they do not believe in themselves.

Rashi explains "their smallness" to mean that their faith was small. But the exact words of the Talmud literally say, "the smallness they had in themselves." Hence, the Rebbe's comment that their main lack **was** that of confidence in themselves.

The Talmud concludes by stating, "there were some among them who did not believe in G-d." If they were Tzadikim, how is this possible? But according to the Rebbe's interpretation, this means that they did not have enough faith in G-d's goodness to believe that they were important to Him.

This is why the Talmud speaks of their "smallness." Their lack of belief was really lack of faith in themselves.

This can also be fitted into Rashi's commentary.

The main lesson here is that you must have faith in yourself.

Believe that even you are dear in the eyes of G-d.

A measure of G-d's goodness is every individual's importance to Him.

Experiencing humility does not mean that you should put yourself into a state of constricted conciousness, but rather that you should constantly ask G-d to help you achieve true humbleness. [This is discussed at length in the second part of *Lekutey Moharan* #22 and #72.]

Shortly after the Rebbe taught the above lesson, he gave another lesson on the section of the *Zohar* beginning, "Rabbi Shimon rejoiced."[86] This appears in *Lekutey Moharan* #61. There he states that Tzadikim suffer from opposition because of their lack of faith in themselves.[87]

32   In *Lekutey Moharan* #205, the Rebbe states that the remedy for the spiritual damage caused by a nocturnal pollution is to say Ten Psalms.

In the second section, #92, these Ten Psalms are specified.

Rabbi Nathan writes:

I was not with the Rebbe when he first revealed the concept brought in lesson #205. But G-d was with me and I came there shortly afterward and heard the entire lesson from someone exactly as the Rebbe had taught it. I then had the opportunity to discuss it with the Rebbe himself, and he reviewed it for me as it is brought in *Lekutey Moharan.*[88]

When the Rebbe first revealed this, he prescribed the remedy of the ten Psalms without specifying which ten must be said. He said, "The exact ten Psalms should be specified. However, any ten constitute the remedy, since any ten Psalms correspond to the ten types of song. These ten melodies are the true remedy."

86   *Zohar* 2:128a.
87   *Lekutey Moharan* 61:5.
88   This took place on Friday, 17 Sivan, 5565 (June 14, 1805) Rabbi Nathan had returned to Breslov eight days after Shavuos, and was told about this by Rabbi Yoske, the husband of the Rebbe's daughter Udel. This was the same day that the first manuscript of *Lekutey Moharan* was given to be bound. *Yemey Moharanat* 8b, *Chayay Moharan* 15a, *LeChochmah* 205.

Before speaking of the Psalms, the Rebbe said, "The first remedy is Mikvah. *Das ersht is Mikvah.* You must first immerse yourself in a Mikvah." He then spoke of the Ten Psalms.

Another time the Rebbe said, "You must be very careful to immerse in a Mikvah on the same day that you have an unclean experience. If you cannot immerse the first thing in the morning, do so any time during the day, even toward evening. It is most important to immerse on the very same day."

[At the end of *Sipurey Maasios* it is brought that he said that it is best to immerse immediately.[89]]

Four long years then passed, and what happened would consume many volumes. It was during this interval that the Rebbe contracted the illness that would eventually take his life. It was also during this time that he travelled to Lemberg (Lvov).

One winter night we stood around him as he lay in bed. Suddenly he began to speak of the Ten Psalms. He told me to get a piece of paper and write down verses alluding to the ten types of song. He then revealed the ten verses, dictating them as they appear in the second section of *Lekutey Moharan* #92.

The Rebbe expressed his desire to specify the Ten Psalms that must be said on the day one has an unclean experience. We stood there waiting, but were not worthy to hear them at that time. We then left.

When I returned for a Sabbath, I happened to see a manuscript where the Rebbe himself had written down the Ten Psalms. I did not think it proper to take the manuscript without permission. I attempted to memorize it, but was prevented by the fear that the Rebbe would mind me entering the room and seeing the manuscript without his permission.

[This took place on *Shabbos Shekalim* 5570 (1810). When the Rebbe left his room to hear the reading of the Torah, I entered and saw the Manuscript.[90]]

On Sunday I went in to take leave of the Rebbe before going home. I asked him to disclose the Ten Psalms, knowing full well that he had already written them down. But the Rebbe demurred, saying that there would be another time. I then left for home without learning them.

A short time later [91] while I was home in Nemerov, the Rebbe revealed the Ten Psalms to the Rabbi

---

90   This would be on 27 Adar I, 5570 (March 3, 1810). *Parparos Lechochmah* B 92 challenges this on the basis that it would be almost five years after the initial revelation, while above it states that it was "close to five years." He suggested that 5570 might be a printing error, and that the actual year was 5569. *Shabbos Shekalim* that year fell on 25 Shevat (Feb. 12 1809). An alternative suggestion is that the "winter night" occurred a year before this *Shabbos Shekalim*. See following note.

91   According to *Parparos LeChochmah*, end of B 5, this took place close to Passover 5569. He writes, that there is a question whether it was before or after the holiday. However, in a letter, Rabbi Nachman of Tulchin, a disciple of Rabbi Nathan, writes that it was revealed between the lesson appearing in *Lekutey Moharan* B 74, and the story of the Seven Beggars, shortly before the Rebbe left Breslov for Uman. (Unnumbered letter, dated Monday, 18 Adar, 5633, at the end of *Alim LeTrufah*.) This sets the year as 5570. The lesson deals with Parshas Parah and most probably was revealed on that Sabbath, 18 Adar II (March 23, 1810). The story of the Seven Beggars was begun on 25 Adar II (March 30), also on a Friday night, as discussed below, note 496. The Ten Psalms were therefore revealed during the intermediate week.

of Breslov [92] and my good friend Reb Naftali of Neme-rov.[93]

The Rebbe asked them to bear witness and said, "Everyone experiences a nocturnal emission at one time or another. I call you to bear witness that these Ten Psalms are a beneficial remedy for this unclean experience. They are an absolute remedy.

"Some people experience such an emission because of overindulgence in food and drink or because of exhaustion and fatigue. Others experience it because of the position in which they happen to be sleeping. In such cases there is no reason for concern. [It is nothing more than bedwetting on the part of an infant.]

"Others are guarded from on high and are protected from such experiences. Still others are spared because of their destiny. A man might dream that he is falling and be awakened by his dream. This is also a sign that he is protected from on high.

"But others experience emissions because of their evil thoughts. This literally creates evil forces of the Husks. [94] But even in this case, saying the Ten Psalms will do much to remedy the spiritual damage.

"Many great Tzadikim sought this remedy and worked hard to find it. Some never had any idea at

92   Although Rabbi Nachman was spiritual leader of Breslov, the one consulted for ritual matters was Rabbi Aaron, son of Rabbi Moshe of Karsin. It was the Rebbe who brought him to Breslov to be Rabbi of the city. *Tovos Zichronos* #7. Rabbi Aaron's great-grandson, Rabbi Yisroel Abba Rosenfeld, was the founder of Breslover Chassidim in America and the first president of the Breslov Yeshiva in Jerusalem. The latter's son, Rabbi Zvi Aryeh Rosenfeld, is one of the leaders of the world Breslov scene.

93   Reb Naftali was a childhood friend of Rabbi Nathan, and was with him when he first met the Rebbe. *Avanehah Barzel* p. 9 (#6).

94   See *Parparos LeChochmah* B 92; *Reshis Chochmah, Shaar HaKedushah* 17. Cf. *Kesubos* 46a, *Avodah Zara* 20b.

all of the true remedy. Others began to perceive it, only to be taken from the world before they could grasp it completely. This is entirely new and is a wonderful and awesome remedy.

"If you can immerse in a Mikvah and then say the Ten Psalms it is certainly best. But even if you are sick or travelling and cannot immerse, saying the Psalms alone is a great remedy.

"If you can say the Psalms with devotion and feeling, it is best. But saying the words alone also helps.

"This remedy has not been revealed since the time of creation.

"I would prefer to do away with this blemish completely, but it is impossible both physically and spiritually. It would involve the permanent change of man's very nature and this is beyond the realm of possibility. Even Moses our teacher and others like him could only change the laws of nature temporarily and then only in specific instances. Even such great miracles as the splitting of the Red Sea and the Jordan were only temporary miracles.

"To do away with this would involve a general alteration of man's nature. This would involve changing every single human being for all time. This is physically impossible. Spiritually this is also impossible. . . .

"These Ten Psalms, however, are a most wonderful and precious remedy.

"Bear witness to my words. When my days are over and I leave this world, I will still intercede for anyone who comes to my grave, says these Ten Psalms and gives a penny to charity. No matter how great his sins, I will do everything in my power, spanning

the length and breadth of the creation to cleanse and
protect him. . . . [95]

"I am very positive in everything I say. But I am
most positive in regard to the great benefit of these
Ten Psalms.

"These are the Ten Psalms: Psalms 16, 32, 41, 42,
59, 77, 90, 105, 137, 150."

These Psalms have been published numerous times.
[However, in the first edition of *Sippurey Maasios,*
because of a printing error, another psalm was er-
roniously substituted for Psalm 137. This error spread
to a number of other published works.]

The Ten Psalms should be recited in the order
that they appear in the Bible.

The Rebbe also said, "This is the *Tikun HaKelali*
—the general remedy. There is a specific remedy for
each sin, but this is the general remedy.

"Go out and spread the teaching of the Ten Psalms
to all men.

"It may seem like an easy thing to say Ten Psalms.
But it will actually be very dificult in practice."

The Rebbe's last words literally came true. We
have suffered much opposition and this has prevented
the world at large from using this remedy. But the
Rebbe had already predicted this.

We have done everything in our power to teach
this remedy to all who wish to use it. Let every man
do as he sees fit. Listen if you want to, or ignore it
if you will. Our own souls we have saved. [96]

95   In *Chayay Moharan* 45a (#41), the following words are
added· "I will pull him by his *Peyos* out of Gehenom."
96   Ezek. 3:18.

The author of *Tikkun Shabbos* attributes these Ten Psalms to a work called *Asarah Hillulim*. This is an error. In *Tikun Moed* they are explicitly attributed to "our master, Rabbi Nachman of blessed memory." Many other authors also attribute these Ten Psalms to the Rebbe.

If you carefully examine all works quoting the Ten Psalms without mentioning the Rebbe, you will find that they were all published after his death, which took place in 5571 (1810) during Succos.[97] However, the above author might have attributed it to another source because of great opposition that the Rebbe suffered. He may have wanted the greatest possible number of people to be able to use the remedy, and therefore took advantage of the Talmudic dictum that it is permissible to alter the truth for the sake of peace.[98] This is especially true in the case of something as important as this remedy.

But we have already mentioned that this is an absolutely new remedy and was never revealed since the beginning of time. Therefore attribute this remedy to the Rebbe so that his lips should murmur it,[99] for this is something that all Tzadikim desire.

For disclosing all this, may we be protected from all sin and harm through the Rebbe's merit, and may we be worthy of a true correction and salvation. Amen —may it be G-d's will.

33. The 13th story in *Sipurey Maasios* is the tale of the Seven Beggars. It was told over a period of several days. Each part of the story alluded to some discussion preceding its telling.

---

97   Rabbi Nachman passed away on Tuesday, the fourth day of Succos. 18 Tishrei (Oct. 16, 1810).

98   *Yebamos* 65b.

99   *Sanhedrin* 90b.

(The story speaks of a boy and girl, lost in the woods, who meet seven beggars. Each of these beggars appears to have a deformity, blindness, deafness, stuttering, a crooked neck, a hunchback, deformed hands and crippled feet. Later the boy and girl marry each other, and on seven successive days each of these beggars tells his story. They each demonstrate that their apparent deformity is really an illusion, masking a unique capability.)

The Rebbe began telling the story on a Friday night.[100] It all began because of a snuff box that one of his followers sent him. I had written to one of my friends about this snuff box and told him to remain happy.

The Rebbe saw this letter and remarked, "I will tell you how people once used to rejoice![101] He then began the story.

He then told the beginning of the story, continuing until the end of the first day of the wedding where they speak to the Blind Beggar.

All this occurred on a Friday night while I was home in Nemerov. On the next Tuesday, my friend[102] came to my house and repeated the story. I was so astonished, I stood there trembling.[103] I had heard many stories from the Rebbe, but I had never heard anything like this.

---

100   This was on 25 Adar II, 5570 (March 30, 1810). *Chayay Moharan* 15b, *Yemey Moharnat* 31b.

101.   In *Chayay Moharan* 16a (#4), the following is added: "What do you know of religion in the midst of your depressed state. I will tell you how people once rejoiced!"

102   This was Reb Naftali. *Yemey Moharnat, loc. cit.* This entire episode is also told there.

103   Dan. 10:11.

I immediately travelled to Breslov, but when I came to the Rebbe's house that night, he was already closed up in his room.

On Wednesday morning I went in to see the Rebbe and spoke with him at length. I told him some news about the surrounding areas, and then brought up the subject of the story he had begun the previous Friday night.

The Rebbe said that he was anxious to know how the story continues and what happened on each of the seven days of the wedding feast. He also wanted to know what happened to the prince who inherited his kingdom during his father's lifetime, the episode that introduces the story. [Even though the Rebbe was telling the story, he spoke as if he was hearing it himself.]

The Rebbe outlined the entire story for me. On each of the seven days of the wedding feast, one of the beggars blesses the couple and gives them gifts The Rebbe also cleared up the subplot of the seven ancient men who could remember back to the beginning of their existence. This is part of the Blind Beggar's story, and my friend had not told it very clearly.

The Rebbe explained what the Blind Beggar meant when he said, "I remember nothing at all—*Ich gedenk gar nisht*."[500] He told me that this beggar goes back the farthest when he says that he remembers nothing, for this means that he can remember the time when absolutely nothing existed.

I was very anxious for the Rebbe to continue and tell the story of the second day. However, just then the Rebbe's attendant came in and announced that it was time for the Rebbe's meal. He set the table and I had to leave.

After the Rebbe had eaten and taken a short nap, I was able to see him again. I stood before him and told him some current news, especially about Berdichov where I had recently been.[104] I told him how the people there are always worried and in need, especially the rich, who are constantly in debt.

I quoted the verse (Eccl. 3:11), "He has set the world in their heart, so that men cannot find out G-d's deeds, from the beginning to the end."

The Rebbe replied, "Is this not our tale? Where are we holding now?"

Completely taken aback by my great desire to hear the rest, I excitedly replied that we were up to the second day. The Rebbe immediately began, "On the second day, the young couple had a great longing to see the Deaf Beggar . . . . "

The Rebbe told the entire story of the second day on that Wednesday morning.

On Friday night, he told the story of the third and fourth days.

On Sunday, he told about the fifth day.

On the following Tuesday, he completed the tale of the sixth day.

We were standing around the Rebbe after he completed the account of the sixth day. One of us then told him a short anecdote and he remarked, "Is this not the story of the seventh day? It seems that people

---

104 Since the previous summer, Rabbi Nathan had been attending to the Rebbe's business affairs in Berdichov. *Ibid.* 27b. Rabbi Nathan's father also had a large business in Berdichov. *Kochavay Or* p. 9 (#1).

are already telling my story. I would very much like
to complete it."

It was not told at that time, however, and the
Rebbe never completed the story.[105]

34   As mentioned earlier the story of the third
and fourth days was told on a Friday night. The Rebbe
was suffering great anguish because his young grandson
was very seriously ill.[106] The grandson was his daughter
Udel's child, and she had already suffered very much
from the loss of other children.[107]

The Rebbe was greatly troubled when he came to
the table that Friday night. He finished the meal very
quickly and concluded with the Grace before the usual
crowd had a chance to arrive.

He remained seated after the Grace and began
to speak. The entire talk dealt with his great anguish
and contained very deep ideas. To the best of our
recollection, it dealt with the "heart that is pursued."[108]

In the middle of his discussion, he suddenly remarked, "Where are we in the story?" I was taken
aback and excitedly answered that we were up to the
third day. The Rebbe began, "On the third day the
couple remembered . . . " and completed the story of

105   The Rebbe himself said that he would tell no more. *Sipurey
Maasios* 77b. On the way from Breslov to Uman, he said, "We will
not be worthy of hearing the end until the Messiah comes." *Yemey
Moharnat* 32b. See *Kochavay Or* p. 96.

106   This was 3 Nissan (April 6, 1810). The child died exactly
one week later. *Yemey Moharnat loc. cit.*

107   She had previously lost several daughters. *Ibid.* 31a, *Avanehah
Barzel* p. 22 (#7). She eventually had two children, Avraham Dov and
Rivka Miriam. *Ibid.* p. 33 (#43); *Alim Letrufah,* unnumbered letter
at end, dated Monday, *Ekev,* 5587.

108   This is in the story of the third day, *Sipurey Maasios* 71a.

the third day. He ended the story by saying, "They
rejoiced very much—*Zei haben a hiloa getan.*"[109]

The Rebbe immediately told the story of the fourth
day. As soon as he finished, he quickly left the table.

I immediately reviewed these stories with the
others who were there in order that not one word be
forgotten. I was so involved in reviewing these remarkable tales that I completely forgot the Rebbe's earlier
discourse, "Woe for what is lost and cannot be
replaced."[110] But thank G-d that we retained the stories
and were worthy of preserving them. For as inspired
as I ever may be, I cannot put their awesome significance into words.

(That Sunday, we were standing around the Rebbe
listening to him speak. He said a sharp word about a
certain group, leading to a conversation about broad
shoulders. This in turn led the Rebbe to ask where we
were in the story. He then told the story of the fifth
day.)[111]

It was very close to Pesach, and the Rebbe's
house was being plastered. On Tuesday he left his house
and stayed with the Rabbi. As we stood around him,
someone told an anecdote. I do not remember it exactly,
but it was related to the story of the sixth day, which
the Rebbe then told. After this, another anecdote was
told, relating to the story of the seventh day, as discussed earlier.

The story of the sixth day was told very close to
Pesach, and in my opinion, the ten walls of the water

---

109   *Ibid.* 72a.
110   *Sanhedrin* 111a.
111   This is emmended from *Chayay Moharan* 16a (#3).

castle mentioned there[112] are related to the splitting of the Red Sea. In my work *Lekutey Halachos*,[113] I have recorded what G-d has enlightened my eyes to see in this story.

Each tale came to be told because of a conversation regarding current happenings in the world. A news item would contain some idea related to a story the Rebbe had in mind, and would lead him to tell it. The news would be the "awakening from below,"[114] drawing an aspect of G-dliness down to be clothed in a particular tale.

This was true of every single story. It was also true of many lessons that the Rebbe revealed when it was not a regular time for followers to come together with him.[115]

In all this we saw the awesomeness of G-d and the greatness of the Tzadik, where everything in the world can be expressed as words of Torah and a revelation of G-dliness. But above all, we saw this in the Tale of the Seven Beggars. This story contains wondrous awesome concepts without end. Read this story carefully. If you truly open your eyes and heart, you yourself will see the lofty teachings in each of the beggars' stories.

Look carefully and you will also see the unique holiness of each of the seven beggars. The Blind Beggar boasts that he does not look upon anything in this world, and is therefore literally blind to all worldly

112   *Sipurey Maasios* 77a.
113   "A Gathering of Laws," (*Yoreh Deah*) *Tolaim* 4.
114   *Zohar* 1:35a, 82b, 88a, 210a, 3:8b. Cf. *Yoma* 39a. Also see *Yemey Moharnat* 41a.
115   The regular times were Rosh HaShanah, the Sabbath of Chanukah, and Shavuos in Breslov, and *Shabbos Shirah*, another Sabbath, and *Shabbos Nachmu* in other cities. *Chayay Moharan* 30a (#24), *Kochavay Or* 37a.

things. The Deaf Beggar cannot hear any worldly
sounds. The same is true of all the beggars.

Read the story carefully. Every word opens new
doors, shedding light on a host of fascinating worlds.
Our limited intellect may not be capable of comprehend-
ing it all, but even what we can understand is remarkable. Then remember that this entire revelation came
about through an anecdote dealing with worldly
affairs. G-d was with us and revealed all this so that
there be good for us and our children forever.

The Rebbe said, "It is best not even to hint at
the mysteries contained in the stories. For when something is completely hidden, it can accomplish the most."

Still, the Rebbe revealed some of the mysteries
contained in his tales, in order that people realize
that they must probe even more deeply.

35   The Rebbe told us about his youth when he
once visited Rabbi . . . . .

He said, "I had not yet attained my present level,
where I could speak to a group and still literally be
involved in the Torah and attached to G-d.

"You think that everything comes at once. This
is far from the truth. You must work and toil before
you can achieve any good quality."

At that point in his youth, it was very difficult for
the Rebbe to lead a group because he wished always to
be involved in his devotions.

Many times when his unique qualities were mentioned, the Rebbe would say, "But I struggled very much
for it. I fasted very much . . . . *Ich hab aber zeir geharivit.
Ich hab asach gefast . . .* "

36   I once heard the following from the Rebbe :[116]

I saw a new angel today.

I know his name and his deputies.

These angels are all holding Shofars.

They first blow a long *Tekiah,* then a staccato *Teruah,* and finally, another *Tekiah.*

These angels seek out lost things.

Many things are lost. [This is because of desire.]

It is written (Ps. 112:10), "The desire of the wicked shall be lost."

The mnemotic for *Tekiah, TeRuah, Tekiah* is T.R.T.

The initial letters of the words in this verse are the same as the mnemotic:

The desire	*Taavos*	*Tekiah*	(long note)
of the wicked	*Rashaim*	*Teruah*	(staccato)
shall be lost	*Toved*	*Tekiah*	(long note)

It is also written (Ps. 83:18), "They shall search and be lost." Even a Tzadik who searches after lost things is himself sometimes lost.

Thus it is written (Eccl. 7:15), "There is a Tzadik who is lost through his righteousness."

The Tzadik must then repent for the sin that was responsible for the loss.

Although the sin was not actually committed by the Tzadik, he is still tainted by it.

When he repents for that infinitesimal taint of sin, he is then able to recover awesome things that have been lost.

When these are found, there is a great tumult and joy on high.

---

[116]   This is also brought in *Lekutey Moharan* B 88. See *Lekutey Halachos (Orech Chaim) Birkas HaPeros* 5, *Alim LeTerufah* 64.

The Rebbe then said, "It is very difficult to receive alms."

It appears that a person who receives alms can do much damage and make it difficult to recover lost things.

They can also cause things to become lost.

It is my impression that the Rebbe's words here are awesomely deep. See what he writes in chapter 88 of the second part of *Lekutey Moharan*. He states there that the concepts of the month of Elul are very helpful for the blemish of the covenant that results from sexual sins. He also speaks of the mystery of unripe fruit. All this is related to the above.

I explicitly heard this from the Rebbe's holy lips, and no one among us has begun to fathom its depth.

37. The Rebbe said, "People bring money to a man as a *Pidyon* or Redemption and ask that he intercede for them on high. They tell him their illness and suffering and other problems. It is a wonder to me that the man accepting the Redemption does not suffer as much as the sick person himself . . . "

From this we can understand that the Rebbe actually felt the pain and suffering of the sick for whom he prayed. He literally felt their every ache and pain.

The Rebbe discussed this many times. He said, "When I first began, I asked G-d to let me feel the pain and suffering of others.

"Sometimes a person would come to me and tell me his troubles, but I would feel absolutely nothing. But I prayed to G-d that I should feel this Jewish suffering. Now I can feel the suffering of another even more than he himself can.

"Another man can forget his own suffering by

thinking of other things. But I concentrated on it very deeply, until I literally bled because of his pain.''

Once one of his followers asked the Rebbe not to forget him. The Rebbe replied, ''How can I forget you? Don't you realize that each one of you has a place in my heart?''

38 . The Rebbe once came inside and said, ''What do you do when a great mountain of fire stands before you?

''A very great treasure lies on the other side.

''The treasure cannot be reached without passing through this fiery mountain.

''And you have no choice but to reach the precious treasure. . . . ''

After several days, the Rebbe spoke about this again.

He said, ''It has already been revealed to me what must be done in such a case.''[117]

39   The Rebbe said that one must use the same powers with money as he does with food. (These powers are acceptance, retention, digestion, distribution, and expulsion.)

When you eat, you make use of your power of acceptance

You also make use of your power of retention, holding the food so that it does not immediately leave your body.

You then use your faculty of digestion and distribution, delivering the food to all parts of the body. The brain receives the choicest parts, with the next best going to the heart. Each part of the body receives what is best for it.

117   See *Succah* 52a.

Following this, you make use of your power of expulsion, excreting the unusable portion of the food. All this is well known.

Money requires these same powers.

You must use your power of retention and not spend the money immediately.

[Not like those who have a great desire for money and spend their life acquiring it, only to squander it immediately.]

You must then make use of your power of distribution, budgeting your income for all your necessities.

It is the same as with food. The choicest portion must be given to charity. The rest must be properly distributed, just as in the case of food.

The Baal Shem Tov once explained why he accepted money from the wicked. He said, "I distribute all the money that I receive. That which comes from the righteous is spent on the needs of pious wayfarers who visit me. Other moneys are distributed accordingly. But money coming from the wicked is spent for my horses and laborers. The money might be all mixed together, but it is automatically distributed in such a manner."

The Baal Shem Tov was able to distribute his income automatically. The same was true of his power of expulsion. The unusable portion of his income was expelled and used for common laborers and horses.

The Rebbe said, "The passion for riches comes mainly to one who does not have a vessel to receive.

"The same is true of eating. For certainly, if one knows how to eat. . . .

"Desire is mainly for that which is not necessary. The same is true of money. I have a vessel. . . . "

40 The Rebbe said:

There are naked souls[118] that cannot enter a body at all.

These souls are more pitiful than anyone alive.

When a soul is born into this world, it can give birth to children and observe G-d's commandments.

But these naked souls have no way of elevating themselves and are most pitiful.

They cannot accomplish anything on high, and also cannot clothe themselves in a body.

There are also incarnations that have not yet been revealed.

[There are many incarnations mentioned in the sacred works of earlier masters. However, other incarnations have never been revealed at all in this world.]

One's incarnation can also cause him to constantly desire to travel. He makes plans to travel, but they do not materialize, and he ultimately remains at home.

41 The Rebbe was once speaking about strife and said:

Why do people worry when others speak against them?

It is because opposition can cause a person to fall from his level, heaven forbid.

The Talmud teaches us that the Great Assembly wanted to count King Solomon among those who have no portion in the future world. The only thing that saved him was King David's intercession.

We see that they had the power to cast out King Solomon with their words.

It is written in the words of King David (Ps.

118 *Tikuney Zohar* 6 (23b), *Zohar Chadash* 37a. See *Chayay Moharan* 34a (#1), *Alim LeTerufah* 350.

119:161), "Princes have persecuted me for nothing, but my heart trembles at Your word."

"Princes have persecuted me" but I know that it is "for nothing." They can accomplish absolutely nothing with their opposition.

I know this because "my heart trembles at Your word." I still have the fear of heaven, and have not fallen from my level.

This is a sign that their persecution was in vain. "Princes have persecuted me for nothing."

42. A number of people were once praising Rashi's commentaries in the Rebbe's presence. The gist of the conversation was that one should use only Rashi's commentary on the Bible, and not those which follow the philosophers.

[Some Biblical commentaries occasionally abandon the traditional Talmudic and Midrashic interpretation in favor of one agreeing with philosophical teachings. These should be avoided. The only necessary commentary is that of Rashi.]

The Rebbe then remarked, "You may not realize it, but Rashi is like the Torah's brother. Every Jew, from childhood on, studies both the written and oral Torah with Rashi's commentary. Think of this, and you will understand Rashi's unique greatness."

43. One of the Rebbe's followers was once very sick. He suffered greatly from tremendous pains in his teeth, and was almost on his deathbed. The torture continued to grow worse, increasing without limit, until his agony was beyond description.

This man's face had become very swollen and the doctors had to resort to all sorts of agonizing methods to remove his teeth. His internal organs were also affected, torturing him to the point of death. It was beyond all measure.

The Rebbe spoke to this man and said, "You have suffered the most severe and bitter pains all these years. But it is still better than one burn in Gehenom. One such singe is worse than all this. *Es iz altz besser eider ein brei in Gehennom. Ein brie in Gehenom is ergir derfun.*"

44. The Rebbe said, "Do not let a word of wickedness leave your mouth."

Do not say that you will commit a sin or be wicked, even though you may be joking and have no intention of carrying out your words. The words themselves can do great damage and later compel you to fulfill them. This is true even if they are uttered only as a joke.

It is written that King Jehu said (2 Ki. 10:18), "Ahab served the Baal a little, but Jehu will serve him much." These words were his downfall.

When King Jehu said these words, he had absolutely no intention to commit idolatory. He only said this to trick the Baal worshippers, as explained in the next verse. Still, this was his downfall, and he later committed idolatory.

The Talmud speaks about this and derives the lesson that "a covenant is made with the lips."[119] You should therefore be very careful with what you say.

45   The Rebbe was once speaking to one of his followers. In the midst of their conversation, they heard someone reciting the evening *Maarev* prayer. He was up to *HaShkivenu* and was saying *VeSaknenu beEtza*

Tova MiL'Fanecha—And remedy us with good council from before You.

The Rebbe said to his follower, "See how this man is saying 'remedy us with good council', running through the words. Doesn't he realize that he must say these words with great emotion and feeling, from the very depths of his heart? This is a most precious prayer. You must always beg that G-d have mercy and grant us good council and advice, that we may be worthy of knowing what is right. . . . "

If you truly want to serve G-d, you must understand this well. Plead before G-d and ask that you be worthy of His good council.

46   The Rebbe spoke of the concept of the Evil Eye:[120]

There is power in a glance.

If an evil thought accompanies this glance it can reach another and harm him. The eye is then evil.

The power of sight actually exists and can touch the visualized object.

When the eye is evil, this glance can do actual damage.

It is for this reason that the look of a menstruating woman can cause a mark of blood to appear on a mirror."[121]

The specific remedy for Evil Eye is to smoke the fin of a fish.

---

120   See *Baba Basra* 2b, *Eruvin* 64b, *Rashi a.l.* "*Baal*," *Pesachim* 26b, 50b, *Baba Metzia* 30a; *Zohar* 3:211b. Also see *Avos* 2:11, 5:22.
121   *Ramban* on Lev. 18:19.

Fin is *S'NaPIR*. Turn the letters into numbers, and the Gematria gives you *RA EYiN*, the bad eye:

SNaPIR — Fin		*Ra EYiN* — Bad Eye	
Samech	= 60	*Resh*	= 200
Nun	= 50	*Eyin*	= 70
Peh	= 80	*Eyin*	= 70
Yud	= 10	*Yud*	= 10
Resh	= 200	*Nun*	= 50
	400		400

Especially good for this is a fish called·the *Shelein*. *Shelein* sounds like *Shel Eyen*—"of the eye"—and the similarity of pronunciation indicates a deeper relationship.

I also heard that the Rebbe said that the fin of a *Shelein* fish should be worn by a man or child who has an Evil Eye. This will protect him.

I heard the following from the same source in the name of the Rebbe:

The Ebil eye's power comes from the four hundred men that Esau brought to fight against Jacob.

It is written (Gen. 32:7), that Esau had "four hundred men with him." These four hundred came to place an Evil Eye upon Jacob's camp.

This four hundred is the numerical value of *RA EYiN* — the bad eye. The four hundred men are the source of the Evil Eye.

Four Hundred is also the numerical value of *SNaPIR* — the fin of a fish. This opposes the four hundred men of Esau and protects against the Evil Eye.

The Rebbe also mentioned a number of other things that add up to four hundred.

47. The Rebbe said:

The greater your riches, the further you are from them.

When you only have a little money, you can keep it on your person.

When you acquire more, you must keep it in a strongbox. It is then more distant from you.

When you acquire still more, then you must keep it in the bank. It is yet further from you.

Acquire still more, and your wealth and investments are scattered in other cities and faraway places. They are still further away from you.

The more honor and riches you have, the further away they are.

Great emperors and kings have very great honor, but it is furthest away of all.

The czar's subjects sing his anthem here each evening, while he sits far away in his palace.

The more honor a man has, the further away it is.

This is true of the worldly.

But with Torah and good deeds, the more you have, the closer it is to you."

48. It is much easier to give advice to another.

When you need advice, it is very difficult to give it to yourself.

After much deliberation, you may decide that one way is the best. You have many reasons and arguments to support this. But as soon as you make up your mind, other considerations enter, tearing down the basis of your original decision. Now it seems that the exact opposite is true.

You therefore need advice from another.

Happy is the man who is worthy of G-d's council.

He will then do what is proper and not lose his World in vain, heaven forbid.

49. It had become fairly common for marriage relationships to degenerate and often result in separation and divorce.

One of his followers once spoke to the Rebbe about this.

The Rebbe said, "This is the work of the Evil One. He works very hard to destroy the family life of young men, in order to trap them in his net, heaven forbid.

"The Evil One lies in wait for them while they are young, working to destroy their family life. He destroys their relationship with all sorts of trickery."

The Rebbe then spoke of this at length.

50. The Rebbe often warned us to honor and respect our wives.

He said, "Women have much anguish from their children. They suffer in pregnancy and childbirth and then have the troubles of raising their children. This is besides the many other areas in which they suffer for you.

"You should take this into consideration and honor and respect your wives."

The Talmud teaches us, "Honor your wives that you may have wealth."[122]

It also states, "It is sufficient that they raise our children."[123]

51. People are often very confused as to the best way to serve G-d. Sometimes it seems necessary to act in one manner, but later this appears completely

---

122   *Baba Metzia* 59a.
123   *Yebamos* 63a.

wrong and another method seems best . . . This can cause one to become very confused and disturbed.

The Rebbe said, "Why is it necessary to confuse yourself? Whatever you do, you do. As long as you do not do any evil, heaven forbid. *Vie men tut, tut men. Abie me-tut nit kein schlecht, chas ve-sholom.*"

52. The Rebbe said, "It is good to make a habit of inspiring yourself with a melody.

"There are great concepts included in each holy melody, and they can arouse your heart and draw it toward G-d.

"Even if you cannot sing well, you can still inspire yourself with a melody sung to the best of your ability while alone at home. The loftiness of melody is beyond all measure."

The Rebbe's works contain towering lessons speaking of song.

The Tale of the Seven Beggars[124] also alludes to the importance of melody. The unconscious princess is cured mainly through melody, through the ten categories of song.[125] Understand the depth of this.

The divine soul in every Jew is a princess — a king's daughter.

She is weary and faint because of her sins.

She is held captive by an evil king and is shot with ten poisonous arrows.

Only a great Tzadik has the power to enter every place where the soul has fallen and remove all ten arrows from her.

124   *Sipurey Maasios* 13.
125   *Ibid.* 76b.

In order to heal her, he must be able to discern all ten types of pulsebeat.

He must know all ten categories of song, for her main cure is through melody and joy.

Taking this as a clue, you can understand the entire story. Use it as a means of returning to G-d in truth. "For the main thing is not study, but deeds."

53 It is very good to have a special room set aside for Torah study and prayer. Such a room is especially beneficial for secluded meditation and conversation with G-d.

The Rebbe once said:

54 Sometimes a man is given great wealth. Everyone else envies him. They spend days and years pursuing wealth because of this envy. But in the end they have nothing.

This is all the work of the Evil One. He works hard to make one man rich so that many others should waste their lives envying him. "Heaven help us against this misleading notion."

55 The Rebbe once said to me, "You do speak with people. You probably ask them *what. Du shmust zich ya mit mentchen. Kerst-ti zei tzu fregen vas.*"

He emphasized the word *vas*—what—stressing it in a loud voice from the depths of his heart.

What?

It is fitting to ask people this question.
You do not think about your purpose in life.

What?

You have many vain and foolish complaints and excuses. Your life is filled with confusion and frustration.

After all this: What?
You say that you have reason to be far from G-d.

What?

What will become of you?
What will you do in the end?
What will you answer the One Who sent you?
What do you think?
What are you on earth if not a stranger?
What is your life, if not vanity and emptiness[126]
"a passing shadow, a scattered cloud?"[127]
You know this well.
What do you say?

Place these words well on your heart. Bring them into the depths of your being. Do not ignore them. Turn them over and over and you will save your soul.

56 . The Rebbe once told me, "Everything you see in the world — everything that exists — it is all a test to give man freedom of choice.'

57   Many times the Rebbe said, "We have nothing at all to do — *me hat gar nit tzu tahn*."
The Rebbe said this in relation to his conversations [and many of them have already been printed].
We find in the Talmud that the disciples of Rabbi Ishmael taught, "the words of the Torah should not be like an obligation, but you are not permitted to exempt yourself from them.'
This explains the Rebbe's statement and is wonderful advice to him who understands it even a little.

126   Isa. 30:7.
127   Ps. 144:4.

58 . Every year people say that previous years were better and times are not as good as they were before. . . .

The Rebbe spoke to us about this at length. He said that people might say that things were much cheaper in the good old days, but then again, people did not have as much money as they have now. A simple householder, even one living from charity, spends more today than the wealthy of yesterday.

He said, "The opposite is true. G-d now directs the world better than ever. *Aderaba. Der Eibershter firt heint sheiner die velt.*

59. The Rebbe spoke to us somewhat about the concept that the true goal of knowledge is the realization of one's ignorance. He said that this is true of every area of knowledge. Even though a person may attain the goal of realizing his ignorance, it may only be in one area of knowledge. He must then first begin to work on a higher plane, aspiring to realize his ignorance at this higher level. And no matter how high one reaches, there is still the next step.

Therefore, we never know anything, and still do not attain the true goal. This is a very deep and mysterious concept. We heard more regarding this once after Pesach,[128] and will discuss it elswhere.[129]

60 Once a king sent three of his servants to deliver a secret message to another king in a distant land. On the way, they had to pass through lands that were at war with their king.

---

128 Pesach, 5565. Cf. *Shevachay Moharan* 8a (#42). Although there is a misprint in the date, it can be resolved on the basis of *Chayay Moharan* 7b (#24).
129 *Sichos* 3.

The first messenger was clever enough to conceal his purpose completely. He passed through the hostile land without them ever realizing that he was carrying a secret message.

The second messenger started through the unfriendly country and was discovered. The people realized that he was carrying a secret message and were going to force him to reveal it. But through his wisdom and endurance, he too was able to escape without revealing the message.

The third messenger was also discovered. Realizing that he too was bearing a secret message, they imprisoned him, and subjected him to all kinds of torture. They tortured him in the cruelest ways possible, but despite his great agony, he refused to tell them anything. He withstood the test without yielding his secret.

They finally realized that their tortures were to no avail, and assumed that they were mistaken and he actually had no secret. They let him go, and he passed through their land, delivering his message to the king.

When they returned, everyone had an opinion as to which of the three deserved the greatest reward. Some said that the first was most deserving, for he acted cleverly enough to hide his secret completely. Others gave the most credit to the second, for he had already been discovered, and still was smart enough to escape.

But the king said that the third messenger deserved the greatest reward of them all. He had already been caught in their net. He certainly also wanted to hide his purpose, but he was not successful. After being captured, he underwent every possible torture and torment. If he would have revealed even one secret, he would have received the greatest honors. Still, he withstood the test, revealing nothing. Therefore, his reward is above all the rest.

[Those who comprehend will to some extent understand the parallel.]

DESIRE

61 The main thing is desire and longing. Of course, this alone is not enough, for it must be realized in action . We are taught that one under duress is exempted by G-d, but this is only true when one actually desires not to be exempted.

You may be under duress, but you should not be satisfied with the fact that you are exempt. You must continually long to bring this good desire to fruition. For when you are not willing to be satisfied with the fact that you are under duress, the desire to complete the task is in itself very beneficial. For then, even if you find the task impossible, you have a worthy accomplishment in the desire alone.

62   The Rebbe once quoted the verse (Ps. 31:25), "Be strong and brave, all who hope in G-d."[130]

The Rebbe stressed "all who *hope* in G-d." You may not be worthy of holiness or devotion. But you can still hope. In this way you can be "brave and strong."

No matter what happens, never let anything discourage you. [131]

You should also encourage others not to be dismayed, no matter what happens. You may be aware of your own failings, but still, this should not prevent you from encouraging others. It is easier to inspire

130   The verse is actually, "be strong and let your hearts be brave." The expression "be strong and brave," as quoted here, is from Deut. 31:6, Josh. 10:25, and 2 Chr. 32:7.

131 ; *Lekutey Moharan* 282, B 78.

others than to strengthen yourself. Thus, our Rabbis teach us, "A prisoner cannot free himself."[132]

There is nothing worse than discouragement. It is written (Deut. 20:3), "do not be afraid or terrified." The Talmud interprets this, "do not be afraid" of the hordes of troops — "nor terrified" of the sound of the war horn."[133]

If you want to be religious, you will also encounter many battles. You will have to be brave in the face of "hordes of troops and the sound of war horns."

You will have to face many such things.[134] You must take a stand and not surrender your ground, no matter what you encounter. Anticipate G-d's help[135] and do not stray from Him.

The Talmud says, "Retreat is the beginning of defeat."[136]

How can you run from G-d? It is written (Ps. 139:7) "Where can I flee from You? If I mount up to heaven, You are there—if I descend to hell, You are there too."

You must be very stubborn in your devotion.[137]

You may feel far from G-d, but do not discourage others. Do just the opposite, and strengthen them in every way you can. Speak to them with words that restore the soul.[138] Do this, and you will also eventually be affected and be worthy of true devotion to G-d.

---

132   Berachos 5b.
133   *Sotah* 8:1 (42a), according to Rashi. Cf. Deut. 31:6.
134   Cf. *Lekutey Halachos (Yoreh Deah) Giluach* 3:9.
135   *Shabbos* 31a.
136   *Sotah* 44b.
137   Cf. *Lekutey Moharan* 48, 51; *Lekutey Halachos (Orech Chaim) Tefillah* 5:43, *Birkas HaMazon* 4:12, *(Yoreh Deah) Basar VeChalav* 5:29, *Shiluach HaKan* 4:2; *Nachalay Emunah* 34.
138   Ps. 19:8.

63   The Rebbe once said, "Thirst is a very great desire."

He wanted to give us some idea of the longing and yearning that is the wondrous thirst for G-d.

The more thirsty you are, the greater your pleasure in drinking water.

Your thirst is the source of your enjoyment.

The same is true of your holy thirst for G-d.

This is the delight of the Future World.

It will be a time of desire and longing.

This is the desire of all desires.[139]

It is the desire through which Moses died.[140]

It is written (Gen. 23:16) that for his final resting place, Abraham paid "four-hundred Shekels of silver."

The holy Zohar says that these are the four-hundred worlds of *yearning* that the just will inherit in the Future World. [141]

They are worlds particularly of yearning. For we will then be worthy of the true yearning and thirst for G-d.

Quenching this thirst will then be the main delight of the Future World.[142]

64   The Rebbe once emphasized the importance of longing and thirsting for the holy. Even if you are not worthy of actual fulfillment, the yearning itself is good.

The Rebbe brought proof for this from a law in the *Shulchan Aruch*.[143] If you are in an unclean place

---

139   *Zohar* 2:88b.
140   *Ibid. Lekutey Moharan* 4:9.
141   *Zohar* 1:123b.
142   Cf. Ps. 39:6, 66:12.
143   *Orech Chaim* 62:4.

and cannot recite the *Sh'ma,* you should at least think about it.

The commentaries[144] explain that you should think that you must recite the *Sh'ma,* and are suffering because of your inability to do so. You then receive the same merit as you would for actually reciting it.[145]

Even though you cannot actually complete an observance, the yearning and longing is still very precious and worthy of reward.

---

144 *Magen Avraham* 62:2
145 *Perishah Ibid.*

FAITH

65 Strengthen yourself in faith, completely avoiding all speculation. Do not engage in philosophy, but believe in G-d with innocent faith.

It may seem that the average person is very far from philosophical involvement, but many embrace it to some degree. Everybody philosophizes. Even young children often have confusing theories.

You must carefully remove all speculation from your heart. Cast it away and do not think about it at all. All you need is a pure faith in G-d and in the true Tzadikim.

We have received the Torah through Moses our teacher, and it has been transmitted to us by the awesome Tzadikim of each generation. There is no question as to their integrity and they can be relied upon without question. All one must do is follow in their footsteps, believing in G-d with innocent simplicity, and keeping commandments of the Torah as taught by our holy ancestors.

When a person is sincere and unquestioning, then he can be worthy that G-d illuminate him with the aspect of Desire, which is even higher than Wisdom[146]

The attribute of Wisdom is actually higher than Faith[147] Still one must avoid the wisdom of speculation

---

146 The Kabbalists speak of Desire as an aspect of *Kesser*, the Crown of creation. See *Shaarey Orah* #10, *Pardes Rimonim* 23:20. This is above the Sefirah of *Chochmah*, Wisdom.

147 The highest aspect of faith is related to *Binah*—Understanding—the Sefirah below *Chochmah*. *Tikuney Zohar*, int. (5a) on Isa. 33:6.

and rely on faith alone. Faith has great power, and when one follows its path, he can achieve Desire, a level even higher than Wisdom.

When one is worthy of Desire, he feels a great longing and yearning toward G-d. This feeling becomes so intense that he does not know what to do. And he cries out.....

But there is a philosopher in every man's heart. He is the Evil One, who raises questions in one's mind. We must humble him and eject him, strengthening ourselves in faith and emptying the heart of all questions.

66   Another time when the Rebbe was discussing faith he remarked, "The world considers faith a minor thing. But I consider it an extremely great thing.

"The main road to faith is empty of all sophistication and speculation. It is the innocent faith of the most average religious person."

67   Atheism is called a burden.

In the verse (Deut. 1:12), "How can I alone bear your encumberance and your burden," Rashi explains that "burden" refers to the fact that there were non-believers among the Jews in the wilderness.

When a person travels to a Tzadik, he casts aside this heavy burden. Travelling to a Tzadik is an act of faith, the opposite of disbelief.[148]

68   If you have faith, you are truly alive.

When you have faith, every day is filled with good.

---

148   See *Lekutey Halachos* (*Choshen Mishpat*) *Chalukas Shutfin* 2:3, 4:5, 5:7.

When things go well, it is certainly good. But when you have troubles, it is also good. For you know that G-d will eventually have mercy, and the end will be good. Everything must be good, for it all comes from G-d.

The man without faith is not really alive. Evil befalls him and he loses all hope. There is nothing to cheer or comfort him, for he has no faith. He is outside of G-d's providence, and has no good at all.

But if you have faith, your life will be good and pleasant.

69 Regarding the Messianic age, it is written (Isa. 4:3), "And it will be, that he who is left in Zion, and he who remains in Jerusalem, 'holy' shall be said to him." The Talmud teaches us that the angels will chant "holy, holy, holy" before the Tzadikim, just like they do before G-d.[149]

This is the plain meaning of the verse. For the Tzadikim who remain faithful before the Messiah's coming, will deserve this, and much more. So difficult will it be to remain firm in faith and not be misled by every one's mistaken beliefs in the pre-Messianic era.

At that time many who call themselves religious leaders will preach falsehood. A group like ours, where people gather together thirsting for G-d's word, will certainly no longer exist. There will remain some truly religious individuals, but they will be very widely scattered.

The Rebbe then quoted the verse (Ex. 17:14), "write this as a record in a book." In days to come, let people know that there was one who already pre-

---

[149] *Baba Basra* 75b. Cf. Isa. 6:3.

dicted this.   Then they will know and be encouraged in their faith in G-d and the true Tzadikim.

70 When you have doubts about your faith in G-d, say out loud, "I believe in perfect faith that G-d is One—first, last and always."

The Evil Urge comes from the fallen Strength.[150]

There is Strength of Holiness that can counteract the Strength of the Husks. [151]

It is written (Ps. 145:11), "And they shall *speak* of Your *strength.*" Speech is holy Strength.

Therefore, when you say "I believe" as above, you awaken the Strength of Holiness. This will offset your doubts, which come from the Strength of the Husks.

The Talmud teaches us, "One should always *agitate* his Good Urge against his Evil Urge.[152]" You should use your Holy Strength to offset the Strength of the Husks.

The Talmud also teaches us that one who does not want to become *agitated* should *speak* calmly.[153] Speaking calmly wards off agitation.

Stillness offsets agitation.

But speaking out loud is in the category of *agitation* which is Strength.

71 It is written (Deut. 4:39), "Know this day and consider it in your heart. . . ." Some philosophers try to use this verse to prove that one must know G-d philosophically. The Rebbe said that this is absolutely false and there is a reference that states that this interpretation was first used by Karaites.

---

150   *Gevuros,* the power of Strength, as opposed to *Chasadim,* the power of Kindness.
151   *Klipos,* the evil husks, as opposed to the good kernel.

152   *Berachos* 5a.
153   *Taanis* 4a, *Etz Yosef* (in *Eyin Yaakov*) a.l.

The only way to know G-d is through faith. This is the only path to knowledge and perception of G-d's true greatness. Thus it is written (Hos. 2:22), "And I will betroth you to me with faith, and you shall know G-d."

In *Lekutey Halachos*[154] there is also a long discussion explaining clearly that true knowledge of G-d comes only through faith.

There are many passages that tell us to know G-d. It is written (Deut. 4:39), "Know this day and consider it in your heart. . . . " It is also written (1 Chr. 28:9), "Know the G-d of your father." There is also (Ps. 100:3), "Know that the L-rd is G-d."

None of these verses have anything to do with philosophy. Their lesson is that we should constantly know that G-d is there and not forget Him for an instant.[155]

Great kings constantly remind their subjects to know that they have a ruler. This is especailly true of soldiers. They are continuously trained to know their lord and king. His fear must be on their faces[156] in order that they serve him absolutely.

A king's subjects are constantly told, "Know that you have a lord and master." They are not told to philosophize about it, but to keep it in mind and not forget it. They are told to always think of the king and not do anything against his will.

The same is true of the Kingdom of Heaven. We are told, "Know the G-d of your father! Know and do not forget! Know this day and consider it in your

---

154 (*Yoreh Deah*) *Giluach* 3:8 ff.
155 Cf. *Sefer HaChinuch* 25.
156 Ex. 20:17.

heart that the L-rd is G-d! Know that the L-rd is G-d!''

We must be reminded of this many times. We might know that ''the L-rd is G-d'' but there are a host of worldly temptations and distractions working to make us forget this. Most people hardly ever think of G-d.

The Bible therefore reminds us, ''Know that the L-rd is G-d! Know the G-d of your father! Take this into your heart and mind until it is tightly bound up there every instant.''

It is therefore written, ''Know this day and consider it in your heart that the L-rd is G-d.'' The main perfection of knowledge is binding your mind to your heart.   You then know ''in your heart that the L-rd is G-d.'' When this enters your heart, you will certainly gain a deep awe of G-d and not sin.

We cannot write further about this, for every man's knowledge of G-d must enter the gates of his own heart.   We can only present enough to enter these gates.

There are no Biblical verses that teach us to know G-d through human speculation built on confused sophistry. Heaven forbid! The only way to know G-d is the way taught by our holy forefathers, who struggled all their lives for Him. They divested themselves of all worldly matters, totally subjugating every desire and emotion. Above all, they achieved total mastery of their sexual drives, releasing themselves from the bondage of the universal root of evil. They were consequently able to perfect their intellect and truly recognize their Creator. This is the heritage they bequeathed us.

It is our duty to accept this heritage with joy. Thus we say in our prayers, ''Happy are we! How good is our portion! How pleasant is our lot! How beautiful is our *heritage*."

The main lesson of these verses is that we take this holy knowledge into our minds, bring it into our hearts and bind it there constantly, "that His fear be on our faces that we sin not. . . . "

72   The Rebbe lived two years after returning from Lemberg. During these last years, he constantly spoke of faith. As we understand him, everything he said was to bring true faith into every Jewish heart.

Many times the Rebbe would remind us of the great favor that Moses our teacher did us by beginning the Torah with the simple words, "In the beginning G-d created the heaven and the earth." He revealed our faith without any sophistication or philosophy.

The Rebbe downgraded all philosophical works, ridiculing them in every possible way. He made it clear to us that the authors of such works knew absolutely nothing. Speaking at length about this, he revealed many wise sayings containing an awesome wondrous truth. Every word was sweeter than honey and the honeycomb,[157] entering the depths of all our hearts.

We have already written about this at length. Some has been published, but it is not even a thousandth of what he said. The way he spoke is also impossible to describe. The words were both sweet and awesome, coming from his lips with holiness, purity, trembling and awe. One could speak to the Rebbe of the most mundane affairs and still bear witness that his words contained all the world's grace.

157   Ps. 19:11.

During the last two years of his life after he
returned from Lemberg, he constantly dwelt on faith.
We could see that every word, both holy and mundane,
was only spoken to bring faith into the world.

It is written (Ps. 119:86), "All your commandments are faith. This is the foundation of the entire
Torah and its commandments."

73   The Rebbe once told someone, "I will tell
you a secret. Great atheism is coming to the world.

"Atheism will come to the world as a test from
on high.

"I know that my followers will be strong and remain
firm in their faith without this, but I am revealing
this to further encourage them. Let them know that
this has already been predicted."

Similar words were heard from the Rebbe's holy
lips many times. With a deep groan we would say,
"Woe! How can a few men stand up against all the
world?"

The Rebbe's words came true. Immediately after
his death, atheism spread in the world as never before
since the beginning of time. The leprous plague began
to flourish in faraway lands where notorious atheists
put together such works as the *Meassef*.[158] This plague
did not spread to our lands until after the passing of

158   "The Gatherer," the first Hebrew literary periodical initiated
by Isaac Eichel, Mendel Bresslau, and the brothers Simon and Zanvel
Friedlander. It was published regularly from 1784 to 1786, and then
sporadically until 1811. Its publishers, the "Society of Friends of the
Hebrew Language," were primarily assimilationists, and only revived Hebrew to introduce Jews to secular culture. Its first contributors were from
Mendelsohn's German school, but it was later dominated by East European
Maskillim. See Waxman, *A History of Jewish Literature* 3:120. Also
see *Machnia Zedim* #4.

the Rebbe and other great Tzadikim. When it reached
our area, the true Tzadikim cried out like a whooping
crane,[159] but none listened to them, for the nonbelievers
already had the upper hand.

Woe is to us! See what has happened in our generation! See the evil decrees that have resulted from
their deeds![160] Woe, what has become of us?

It all came about as the Rebbe predicted with his
holy inspiration. We see that it is still spreading, even
now. Woe, who knows what will be in days to come?

The Rebbe told us many times that this was predicted by the prophets. It was especially predicted
by the prophet Daniel, who said (Dan. 12:10), "Many
will purify themselves and be refined." He told us
that in the End of Days Jews will be refined in faith,
for many will rise up to pervert it. These are the
"enlighteners" and atheists of our generations.

It should be easy to withstand this test, seeing
that it has already been predicted. But the temptation
will be so great that many will stumble and fall to the
depths.

We are writing this so that all who desire the
truth of our holy faith should know that the Rebbe
already predicted this. Let this restore their soul and
strengthen their hearts toward G-d and his holy Torah
as taught by our sages of old.

74 "Where science and philosophy end, that is where
[true wisdom, which is] Kabbalah begins."[161]

---

159   *Kidushin* 44a. Cf. *Targum* on Jer. 8:7
160   This might refer to the *Maskil*, Isaac Baer Levensohn, who
was largely responsible for the harsh conscription laws of 1827. Posner,
The Tzemach Tzedek and the Haskalah Movement (Kehot, N. Y. 1969)
p. 14. He was also responsible for the censorship laws. *Nevey Tzadikim*
p. 102. See also *Chayay Moharan* 4a (#1), 5a (#6), *Kochavay Or* p. 43
(#6). Levinsohn lived in Nemerov and Tulchin in 1822 and 1823.
161   Cf. *Lekutey Halachos* (*Orech Chaim*) *Netilas Yadayim* 6:79.

[Scientists and philosophers can only speculate within the limits of the physical world. They can reach up to the stars and galaxies, but beyond that, they know absolutely nothing. Even their understanding of the physical world is very incomplete, as they themselves admit.

The wisdom of Kaballah begins where their wisdom ends, beyond the physical world.

The Kaballah includes the entire physical world as part of the World of Action. Its teachings then go beyond the World of Action, to the Universe of Formation, Creation and Emanation.[162]

The World of Action also has a spiritual level beyond the realm of science and philosophy. The Kaballah speaks only of the spiritual roots of the World of Action and above. Therefore, the Kaballah begins where scientific knowledge ends.]

75 Speaking of awesome degrees of perception, the Rebbe once said:

The wisdom of philosophy ends with the physical world.

Beyond the stars, it can only imagine G-d's essence.

There are really many levels of worlds beyond this. This truth is only found in the Kabbalah.

It is written (Isa. 40:28), "His understanding cannot be grasped." One who knows the truth of Kabballah well perceives this. For there is level above level[163] . . . .

The Rebbe once saw a book containing writings

---

162 The Kaballah speaks of four transcendental worlds, *Atzilus* (Emanation), *Beriah* (Creation), *Yetzirah* (Formation), and *Asiyah* (Action or Completion), alluded to in Isa. 43:7. See *Pardes Rimonim* 16; *Etz Chaim, Shaar K'lalos ABYA.*

163 Eccl. 5:7.

of the Ari not found elsewhere. This work speaks of the levels of development before the Universe of Emanation contained in the World of the Garment.[164] This is also discussed in the work, *VaYakhel Moshe.*[165]

I was very surprised when the Rebbe told me this. I had thought that there was nothing higher than Emanation and was astonished to discover Kabbalistic teachings speaking of higher levels.

I expressed my surprise to the Rebbe, and he remained silent for a while. Then he said, "Don't you realize that philosophers think that all knowledge ends with the stars? . . . "

This is also the case with True Knowledge. Even in the transcendental worlds there are levels above levels, high above high, without limit or bound.

---

164 *Olom HaMalbush.* Worlds above *Atzilus* are discussed in *Pardes Rimonim* 11, *Etz Chaim, Drush Egolim VeYosher* 4; *Shaar Ha-Hakdamus* 1.

165 "And Moses Assembled," a Kaballistic work by Rabbi Moshe ben Menachem, a disciple of Rabbi David Openheimer of Prague (1664-1737). *Shem HaGedolim.* First published in Dessau in 1699.

JOY

76 When you are always happy, it is easy to set aside some time each day to express your thoughts before G-d with a broken heart. But when you are depressed, it is very difficult to isolate yourself and speak to G-d. You must force yourself always to be happy, especially during prayer[166].

The Rebbe said that true happiness is one of the most difficult things to attain in serving G-d

Another time he said that it seems impossible to achieve happiness without some measure of foolishness. One must resort to all sorts of foolish things if this is the only way to attain happiness[167].

When a person attains true joy, then G-d Himself watches him and protects him from sexual defilement. [168]

77 Heartbreak is in no way related to sadness and depression.

Heartbreak involves the heart, while depression involves the spleen.

Depression comes from the Other Side and is hated by G-d. But a broken heart is very dear and precious to G-d. [169]

It would be very good to be brokenhearted all day. But for the average person, this can easily degenerate into depression.

166   Brechos 25b

167   *Lekutey Moharan B 24, Shevachay Moharan* 4b (#3). Cf. *Zohar* 3:47b, *Pesachim* 117a.

168   *Lekutey Moharan* 169.

169   Cf. Ps. 51:19. See *Shevachay Moharan* 3b (#6, 7).

You should therefore set aside some time each day for heartbreak. You should isolate yourself with a broken heart before G-d for a given time. But the rest of the day should be joyful. [170]

The Rebbe emphasized this many times telling us not to be brokenhearted except for a fixed time each day. He said that we should always be joyful and never depressed.

78   After heartbreak comes joy.

Later happiness is a true sign of a broken heart.

79   Sometimes your prayers may be devoid of enthusiasm. At such times, you must compel your emotions and make your heart burn with the words.

Sometimes one works himself up and actually makes himself angry. People then say, "He creates his own anger — *Er schnitzt zich ein roigez.'*

You must do the same during prayer. Be like the man who makes himself angry. Work yourself up and bring these emotions into your prayers.

The enthusiasm may be forced at first, but it will eventually become real. Your heart will burst aflame with G-d's praise, and you will be worthy of knowing true prayer.

You can make yourself happy in the same way.

You must pray with great joy, even if this happiness is forced. Happiness is always a virtue, but especially during prayer.

If you are disturbed and unhappy, you can at least put on a happy front. Deep down you may be depressed, but if you act happy, you will eventually be worthy of true joy.

170   *Lekutey Moharan* B 24;

This is true of every holy thing. If you have no enthusiasm, put on a front. Act enthusiastic, and the feeling will eventually become genuine. Understand this well.

80. It was my custom to see the Rebbe every year after Simchas Torah. He would always ask me if I truly rejoiced on the festival. Many times he told me how the community celebrated in his house, and how much pleasure he derived from their joy.

Once the Rebbe spoke to me about Simchas Torah in the middle of the year. He asked me, "Do you now feel joy in your heart? Do you feel this happiness at least once a year?"

[G-d was with me and I was able to rejoice with all my heart many times each year. This joy was often so great that words cannot express it. This is the joy of being a Jew, of believing in G-d, and it flows through the gates of every man's heart and cannot be comunicated. Within our group, when we rejoice, even the lowliest one among us experiences a feeling of closeness to G-d that is beyond all description.]

The Rebbe very much wanted us to be joyous all year round, particularly on Simchas Torah, Purim, the Sabbath and festivals.

MEDITATION

81 It is very good to pour out your thoughts[171] before G-d, like a child pleading before his father[172] G-d calls us His children, as it is written (Deut. 14:1), "You are children to the L-rd your G-d." Therefore, it is good to express your thoughts and troubles to G-d, like a child complaining and pestering his father[173]

You may think that you have done so much wrong that you are no longer one of G-d's children, but remember that G-d still calls you His child. [We are taught, "For good or for evil you are always called his children."[174]]

Let us assume that G-d has dismissed you and told you that you are no longer His child. Still you must say, "Let Him do as He wills. I must do my part and still act like His child."

How very good it is, when you can awaken your heart and plead until tears stream from your eyes, and you stand like a little child crying before its Father.

82 My grandfather, Rabbi Nachman Horodenker, of blessed memory, told the following story:

I was once travelling on a ship. We ran out of provisions and were without food for several days. Finally we reached an Arab city, where there were no Jews.

---

171   Ps. 142:3.
172   *Taanis* 3:8 (19a).
173   *Alim LeTerufah* 254.
174   *Kiddushin* 36a.

An Arab took me in and offered me food. I had not eaten for several days, and quickly washed my hands and said the blessing for bread. I was just about to take a bite, when a thought entered my mind: "Do not eat the bread of one with a mean eye![75]"

A random thought is not without meaning, and I did not know what to do. I had aready said the blessing, but I realized the significance of this thought, and was determined not to eat anything of this Arab. Just then another thought entered my mind. "I have commanded the Arabs to feed you.[176]

[When the Rebbe told this story,[177] he commented how proper it was for his grandfather to insist on acting according to this thought. Every thought entering the mind must contain some element of truth.]

You must learn a lesson from my grandfather. A confusing thought may enter your mind, but if you stand firm, G-d will send you another thought to encourage you.

Similarly, you may imagine that you are no longer one of G-d's children. But if you do your part, G-d will eventually send you thoughts of encouragement.

All Israel are called children of G-d. Therefore, you should pour out your thoughts and troubles before G-d, just like a child complaining to his father.

---

175 Prov. 23:6.

176 1 Ki. 17:4. This is usually translated, "I have commanded the ravens to feed you." However, the Hebrew word for ravens, *orvin*, can also be translated as Arabs. Cf. *Radak ad loc.*

177 This story was told after Shavuos, 5569 (1809). *Chayay Moharan* 15b. On that Shavuos Rabbi Nacman had delivered a lesson based on the above verse, appearing in *Lekutey Moharan* B 4. *Yemey Moharnat* 27b, *Parparos LeChochmah ad loc.*

83   You can shout loudly in a "small still voice[178]."
You can scream without anyone hearing you shouting
with this soundless "small still voice."

Anyone can do this. Just imagine the sound of such
a scream in your mind. Depict the shout in your imagination exactly as it would sound. Keep this up until
you are literally screaming with this soundless "small
still voice."

This is actually a scream and not mere imagination.
Just as some vessels bring the sound from your lungs
to your lips, others bring it to the brain. You can
draw the sound through these nerves, literally
bringing it into your head. When you do this, you are
actually shouting inside your brain.

When you picture this scream in your mind, the
sound actually rings inside your brain. You can stand
in a crowded room, screaming in this manner, with
no one hearing you.

Sometimes when you do this, some sound may
escape your lips. The voice, travelling through the
nerves, can also activate the vocal organs. They might
then produce some sound, but it will be very faint.

It is much easier to shout this way without words.
When you wish to express words, it is much more
difficult to hold the voice in the mind and not let any
sound escape. But without words it is much easier[179]

84   It is best to worship as early as possible in
the morning. .

Worshipping early is a sign that one realizes the
great importance of prayer. He does not want to delay

---

178   I Ki. 19:12.

179   This was one of Rabbi Nachman's own practices. *Shevachay
Moharan* 4a (#1). This does not apply to formal prayer, where one
should worship in a loud voice. *Avenehah Berzel* p. 16 (#14).

it, lest something cause him to lose the opportunity completely. He therefore strives to worship as early as he possibly can.

85 One who does not meditate cannot have wisdom.

He may occasionally be able to concentrate, but not for any length of time. His power of concentration remains weak, and cannot be maintained.

One who does not meditate also does not realize the foolishness of the world. But one who has a relaxed and penetrating mind can see that it is all vanity.

Many desire to travel widely and become famous and powerful. They do not have enough perception to realize that this is vanity and striving after the wind.[148] It is all the more foolish because it does not actually result in pleasure even in this world. The main result of such fame is suffering and insults.

One of the Rebbe's followers once had a strong desire to become a renowned religious leader. The Rebbe told him, "You cannot even say the prayer after meals sincerely! Everything you do must be acceptable to others. Never once do you do something for the sake of G-d alone."

86 In lesson #46 in the second part of *Lekutey Moharan,* the Rebbe says that *KaShYa*—difficulty or question—consists of the initial letters of the verse (Ps. 27:7) *"Shma Y--- Koli Ekra*—Hear G-d my voice, I call..." In this lesson it appears that there is something missing before the phrase. "nevertheless G-d hears his voice and this is his salvation."

This lesson teaches us that when you cry out with your heart, this itself is a category of faith.

You may have many questions and grave doubts, but when your heart cries out it shows that you still have the burning spark of faith. Without this spark you would remain still. The cry itself is therefore in the category of faith. Understand this.

This cry can also bring you to faith.

The cry itself is an aspect of faith, but it is a very weak faith. But the cry can bring you to strong faith. It can elevate and strengthen your faith until all difficulties vanish.

Even if you are not worthy of this, the cry itself is still very beneficial.

87. I found this in a manuscript written by a member of our group:

It is best to seclude yourself and meditate in the meadows outside the city.

Go to a grassy field, for the grass will awaken your heart.

88. Reb Naftali told me that he heard the Rebbe say, "A Jewish heart should be drawn to G-d so strongly that every heartbeat is a flame yearning for G-d."

The Rebbe gestured with his hands, expressing this great yearning.

He said, "Even when you sit among others, you can lift your hands along with your heart and cry out to G-d with a yearning soul."

The Rebbe then lifted his hands with great emotion, and with wonderful yearning recited the verse (Ps. 38:22), "Do not forsake me, O L-rd my G-d."

The Rebbe used this as an example, saying that even when you are among others, you can arouse yourself toward G-d with great emotion.

89. One of the Rebbe's followers asked him the difference between depression and a broken heart.

The Rebbe answered, "When you have a broken heart, you can be standing in a crowd and still turn around and say, 'Master of the world. . . .'"

The Rebbe then raised his hands with great emotion and said, "Master of the world."

90. This same man told me that he wanted to speak to the Rebbe many times, but could not open his mouth when he was with him. He found it impossible to tell the Rebbe what was in his heart.

One Friday afternoon the Rebbe went to the Mikvah in honor of the Sabbath as was his custom. This man was attending him and wanted to say something but was unable to open his mouth.

The Rebbe asked him to pass him his shoes. As he lifted the shoes, the Rebbe said, "Make a habit of speaking to G-d. Then you will also be able to speak to me."

The man followed this advice and was soon able to speak to the Rebbe. He still found it very dificult, however, to express himself.

The Rebbe said, "You are like a warrior who girds his loins to overcome a mighty wall. When you come to the gate, you find it blocked with a spider web. Can you imagine anything more foolish than returning in defeat because of a spider web blocking your path?" [The parallel is obvious.]

The main thing is speech. Use it and you will win every battle.

"You can meditate in thought, but the most important thing is to express it in speech."

This parallel teaches a most important lesson. You may find it difficult to speak with G-d.

You might also find it dificult to speak to a true Tzadik.

This difficulty is great foolishness. It is mere laziness and bashfulness and a lack of virtuous boldness.[180]

You are ready to use your speech to overcome the great battle against the evil within you.

You are on the verge of victory and are about to break down walls with your words. The gates are ready to fly open.

Should you then not speak because of mere bashfulness? Should you hold back because of a minor barrier like this?

You are about to break down a wall. Will you be discouraged by a spider web?

This same man told me that the Rebbe prescribed that he spend two hours each day in secluded prayer. For an hour he was to meditate and prepare himself to speak. When his heart was awakened, he was to then speak to G-d for another hour.

91. The Rebbe spoke of encouraging oneself in prayer. No matter what you are, you can strengthen yourself and stubbornly pray to G-d.

The Rebbe said that you should think in the following vein:

I may be far from G-d because of my many sins.

Let it be. If this is so, then there can be no perfect prayer without me.

---

180 *Betza* 25b, *Avos* 5:20, *Lekutey Moharan* 22:4, 147, 271; *Lekutey Halachos* (*Choshen Mishpat*) *Matanah* 5:11, *Maakeh* 4:2.

The Talmud teaches us that every prayer that does not include the sinners of Israel is not a true prayer.[181]

Prayer is like an incense offering. The Torah requires that the incense contain *Chelbonah* (galbanum), even though it has a vile odor by itself.

If I consider myself a sinner, then I am an essential ingredient of every worship service. No prayer is perfect without me.

I, the sinner, must strengthen myself even more to pray to G-d and trust that in His mercy He will accept my prayer. I am the perfection of the prayer— the *Chelbonah* in the incense.

Just like the vile smelling *Chelbonah* is an essential ingredient of the sweet incense, so my tainted prayer is a vital ingredient of the prayers of all Israel. Without it, prayer is deficient, like incense without the *Chelbonah*.

92 . The Rebbe once spoke to one of his disciples about clothing:

He said, "You must pray for everything. If your garment is torn and must be replaced, pray to G-d for a new one. Do this for everything.

"Make it a habit to pray for all your needs, large or small.

"Your main prayers should be for fundamentals, that G-d help you in your devotion, that you be worthy of coming close to Him.

"Still, you should also pray even for trivial things.

"G-d may give you food and clothing and everything else you need even though you do not ask for them. But then you are like an animal.

181   *Kerisus* 6b.

"G-d gives every living thing its bread[590] without being asked. He can also give it to you this way.

"But if you do not draw your life through prayer, then it is like that of a beast. For a *man* must draw all necessities of life from G-d only through prayer."

I once had a slight need for some insignificant thing. When I mentioned it to the Rebbe, he said, "Pray to G-d for it."

I was quite astonished to learn that one must even pray to G-d for such trivial things, especially in a case like this, where it was not even a necessity.

Seeing my surprise, the Rebbe asked me, "Is it beneath your dignity to pray to G-d for a minor thing like this?"

ON TORAH STUDY

93   The Rebbe once spoke about the current print-ing of sacred books. The number of printers had increased, publishing both recent and earlier works. They had no lack of customers, for every one was buying these volumes.

The Rebbe said the Talmud teaches us that "The day will come when the Torah will be forgotten among Jews." Therefore, many books are printed and bought, with people building up their own libraries. Since even the simplest tailor has books, the Torah is not forgotten.

As each book is published, people rush to buy it, building up respectable collections. In this manner the Torah does not fall into oblivion.

What people do not realize is that these books are of no help unless people look into them and study their teachings. But today the Torah has fallen very much, and few people study it. [For how can books prevent the Torah from being forgotten if nobody studies them?]

94   The Rebbe said, "I have a great longing to institute a rule that each person study a fixed amount in our sacred literature each day without fail.

He said that this should even apply to those who are very far from holiness, even those who are caught in the evil trap[187] and sin habitually, heaven forbid. Still, the strength of the Torah is so great that it can free them from their habitual sins.

182   Eccl. 9:12.

If even the worst sinner would take upon himself a set practice to study a fixed amount every day,
he would be able to escape from the evil trap. The
Torah's strength is so great that it can accomplish
everything.[183]

A person's main goal should be to do good and
serve G-d without sophistication. Every good and holy
thing can be done with absolute simplicity. One can
study much Torah, do much good, and spend much time
in prayer, all without sophistication at all.

The Rebbe continually warned us to always be
happy. Much of this discussion is recorded in his holy
works. However, there were countless other times that
he discussed this.

95 In our sacred literature[184] we find that G-d gave
us the power to forget so that we should always appreciate the Torah like the first time we learned it.
Because you forget, you can relearn a lesson or review,
and it is like learning it anew. Therefore, you appreciate
it as much as the first time.

A good illustration is provided by men hired to
fill leaky barrels. The more they pour into the barrels,
the more leaks out.

The fools complain, "Why are we working in vain?
What good is it to fill the barrels if it all leaks out?"

But the wise ones reply, "What difference does it
make? Don't we get paid for every day we work? If the
barrels leak, our wages are not reduced."

---

183 Reb Naftali asked the Rebbe if this applies to actual sinners
and was answered in the affirmative, with a reference to *Tikuney Zohar* 3
(18b). *Sichos Moharan* 35a (#122), See *Zohar* 1:195b; *Lekutey Halachos*
(*Orech Chaim*) *Betzias HaPas* 22.

184 *Koheles Rabbah* 1:34.

The same is true of your sacred studies. You might forget them, but your reward is not reduced. [185]

96   If you want to study with continuous diligence, be careful never to speak against a fellow Jew.[186]

When the bride is beautiful, love is perfect.[187]

But, when the bride is blemished, love cannot be complete.

The Torah is a bride.

It is written (Deut. 33:4), "Moses charged us with the Torah, a heritage for the congregation of Jacob."

The Talmud says: Do not read *MoRaShA*—heritage —but *Me'uRaSa*—the betrothed. "Moses charged us with the Torah, the betrothed of the congregation of Jacob."[188]

Every Jew is a letter in the Torah.

The six hundred thousand letters in the Torah parallel the six hundred thousand Jewish souls.[189] The Torah is the root of all Jewish souls.

If there is a defect in a single Jew, it is also a blemish in the Torah.

But if you are careful not to speak against any Jew, then you will also find the Torah perfectly beautiful.

You will then have a deep love for the Torah, for when the bride is beautiful, love is perfect.

This great love will lead you to great diligence in your studies.

---

[185]   *Avos deRabbi Nathan* 27:3, *VaYikra Rabbah* 19:2.

[186]   This was said on the day before Rosh HaShanah 5571 (Sept. 28, 1810), shortly before the Rebbe's demise. It was given in response to a request for advice on how to achieve diligence in study. *Chayay Moharan* 10a (#34).

[187]   Cf. Cant. 4:7.

[188]   *Berachos* 57a, *Pesachim* 49b.

[189]   *Zohar Chadash, Shir HaShirim* 74d. Cf. *Lekutey Moharan* 2:6, 14:3, 273.

It is written (Ps. 19:8), "G-d's Torah is perfect; it restores the soul."

Each Jew represents a letter in the Torah.

When people neither seek out nor speak of the flaws in their fellow Jews, then the Torah is perfect, with neither flaw nor blemish.

When "G-d's Torah is perfect" then, "it restores the soul."

When people have this great love for the Torah and can sense its true sweetness, then "it restores the soul."

When people find the Torah without fault, then their love makes them worthy of continuous perseverance in its study.

97   The study of *Zohar* is extremely beneficial.

Through studying the *Zohar*, you can attain enthusiasm for all your sacred studies.

The very language of the *Zohar* is so holy, it can motivate you to serve G-d.

The *Zohar* uses most forceful expressions in speaking about our duty toward G-d.

When speaking of a person who does good, the *Zohar* says "*Zakah* . . . Worthy is he!"

On the other hand, it cries out against a sinner, "*Vai*! . . . Woe! Woe is to him! Woe is to the soul who strays from serving G-d!'

Reading such expressions can greatly influence you to serve G-d.

98   When he used it in the *Zohar*, Rabbi Shimon bar Yochai made the Aramaic *Targum* Language so holy that even other things written in this language have the power to arouse a person toward G-d.

99   The Rebbe said that every one of his lessons can be applied to the entire Bible and Oral Torah (that is, the entire literature of the Talmud and Midrash).

100   The Rebbe once spoke to me about innovating original concepts in the Torah.

Speaking with wonder and awe, he said, "From where does one get a new concept? When one is worthy of innovation, his original thoughts are really very wondrous and mysterious. From where do they come?"

An original idea is a revelation of G-d, bringing something from nothingness to existence.

At first you do not know the idea at all.

It still exists within the Infinite in a state of nothingness.

This is the source of all wisdom.

Every new idea is drawn from this source.

We therefore see G-d's revelation in each new idea.

I discussed this with the Rebbe and said, "Don't I know this! Sometimes I must struggle desperately to innovate even a single word." [While at other times the heart is opened and many new ideas pour forth.]

The Rebbe answered, "Even this is a great wonder and mystery."

It may take great effort to come up with even one original word, but even this is one of G-d's miracles. For what is the source of even this one word?

If you have a desire for the truth and a heart to understand, you can literally see the reality of G-d's existence. If you yourself can originate new ideas, you certainly see G-d's revelation in them. But even if you cannot innovate yourself, you can still see G-d's reality and greatness in the wondrous flow of new concepts found in our sacred literature.

It is written (Ps. 19:8), "G-d's witness is faithful."
The holy Torah is a faithful witness of G-d.

This is discussed at length in my work, *Lekutey Halachos.*

101   The Rebbe said, "You may expound the Torah and innovate in any area you wish.

"The only condition is that you may not use your interpretations to innovate or change any law. This is particularly true of innovations based on *Drush* and *Sod,* expositary construction and esoteric resolution."

From what the Rebbe said, we understood that you may expound and innovate according to your intellectual attainment, even in such Kabbalistic works as those of the holy Ari. The only stipulation is that you may not drive any religious practice or law in this manner.

102   The Rebbe was once speaking of the tremendous greatness of the Torah, and, its awesome secrets.
He said, "The entire *Tikuney Zohar* (a work of seventy chapters) is but a commentary on the one word *Berashis,* the first word in the Torah.

"Thousands of volumes would not suffice to explain all the secrets found in the *Tikuney Zohar.*

"Its study has no end. So great is the *Tikuney Zohar* that all the skins of Nevios would not be sufficient to contain its wisdom.

"All this is but a commentary on a single word —*Berashis* (In the beginning).

"Take the next word—*bara*—'He created'. A volume equal to the *Tikuney Zohar* could also be written on it. It would contain an equal number of mysteries.

"Now understand the depth of our Holy Torah.

"A *Tikuney Zohar* could be written on each and

every word. Each one contains inconceivable depth and mystery.

"The Torah contains not one, but many words.

Its greatness is beyond the ability of language to describe."

SIMPLICITY

103　Many times the Rebbe said that no sophistication is needed in serving G-d. All that is required is simplicity, sincerity, and faith.

The Rebbe said that simplicity is the highest possible thing.

G-d is certainly higher than all else. And G-d is ultimately simple.

104　I heard that the Rebbe once said, "my achievements came mainly through simplicity. I spent much time simply conversing with G-d and reciting the Psalms."

This is how he achieved what he did.

He said, "If I only knew that G-d would make me into the unique person that I am today. I would have accomplished in one day what took me an entire year."

[That is, the Rebbe would have been so enthusiastic, he would have done as much in a single day as he used to do in an entire year.]

The Rebbe deeply yearned to serve G-d like the ignorant common people. He often said, "*Ay! Ay! Prustick!* Oh! Oh! Simplicity!"

The Rebbe also said, "I have spoken with many great Tzadikim. They all said that they attained their high level through *Prustick*—absolute simplicity. They would do the simplest things, secluding themselves and conversing with G-d. This is how they attained what they did. Happy are they."

There were many things he told us to do. These

did not involve deep intentions or the unification of the transcendental worlds through *Yechudim*. The things he told those close to him to do were simple acts of piety.

105 The Rebbe told his followers not to fast at all unless he prescribed it.[190]

He might tell one person to fast for a certain interval. To another he might prescribe undertaking a fast from Sabbath to Sabbath. To a third he would say that once a week he should stay awake one night and abstain from eating animal products for twenty-four hours.[191]

There were many whom the Rebbe told to fast on the day before *Rosh Chodesh* (the New Moon).

He also told most of his followers to be careful to immerse in the Mikvah on days associated with festivity when *Tachnun,* the penitential prayer, is not said.[192] He told this to many people.

The Rebbe also told many people to study eighteen chapters of Mishneh every day.[193]

The Rebbe prescribed many courses of study, a different one for each man.

There was one course of study, however, that he prescribed for all, and that was the daily study of the codes. The Rebbe said that even when one has no time, he should still study at least one law in the *Shulchan Aruch* each day, no matter where that law might be. He said that this is an important obligation for every Jew.

190   See *Sichos Moharan* 28a (#45).

191   These practices were actually prescribed for Rabbi Nathan when he first met the Rebbe. *Avanehah Barzel* p. 12 (#9), *Kochavay Or* p. 12 (#4).

192   Cf. *Avanehah Barzel* p. 22 (#6).

193   This also applied to Rabbi Nathan.

Another practice that he universally prescribed was for us to seclude ourselves in prayer each day. He told us to express our thoughts before G-d and ask that He have mercy and allow us to achieve true devotion. This secluded prayer was to be in the language we normally spoke. . . . This is already discussed at length in the Rebbe's printed works.

The Rebbe would specify various practices for each person. He would also change these practices even for a single individual.

For example, the Rebbe might first tell a person to study eighteen chapters of Mishneh each day. After a while, the Rebbe would exempt him from this and prescribe some new practice.[194]

This is how the Rebbe acted toward his followers. He would tell one person to study a particular code each day, while another would be told to study a certain Mishneh every day.

The Rebbe would look at the root of a man's soul and prescribe the practice necessary to correct each blemish. Each person then required a specific practice.

There were other practices that he prescribed for all his followers, as discussed earlier.

Still other practices were prescribed for many people. Others were specific for particular individuals.

The same was true with regard to time.

There were some practices that the Rebbe prescribed for a man's entire lifetime. An example was the codes, which the Rebbe clearly told us to study every day of our life.

194   This apparently also occurred to Rabbi Nathan. On *Shabbos Chanukah*, the Rebbe told him to change his course of study to the codes, and then in the summer, it was changed again to the Kaballah. *Yemey Moharnat* 7b.

In other cases, the Rebbe prescribed a certain practice for a given period of time, and then substituted another routine.

Most of the practices prescribed by the Rebbe seemed very simple. However, they were all prescribed on the basis of awesome hidden mysteries and were very far from simple in their effect. The Rebbe, however, did not reveal any of these mysteries to us. He simply prescribed a routine and did what was necessary with it.

The Rebbe said, "Everything I prescribe is helpful as a remedy both for the past and the future, as well as after death, in the Messianic age, during the resurrection, and in the Future Life."

HIS PARABLES

Treasure or Test

There once lived a poor man who supported himself by digging clay and selling it. One time, while going about his digging, he found a valuable stone. He did not know how much the stone was worth, so he set out to have it appraised. He learned that in his country there was no one with enough money to pay for this stone, so great was its value. Instead, he had to travel to London to find a suitable market.

Being a very poor man, he could hardly afford to make this journey, so he sold all his worldly possessions and went begging from door to door. This gave him sufficient funds for the trip as far as the port. Upon reaching the port, he found that he could not afford to purchase a ticket for the ship sailing for England. He approached the captain and showed him his precious gem. The captain was very pleased and allowed him to board the ship, thinking he must be a very rich and honorable person to possess such a gem. The captain then assigned him to a First Class room and lavished upon him all the services and luxuries rendered to the very wealthy. In this room, there was a window looking out to the ocean. The man rejoiced and exulted in his diamond particularly during his meals, because eating in good spirits is very beneficial to proper digestion.

It happened that once the man fell asleep upon completing his meal, with his diamond on the table before him. The servant entered the room to collect the dishes, and not noticing the diamond, shook the tablecloth out of the window into the ocean. When the man awoke and realized his misfortune he was so upset that he nearly lost his mind. What would the captain do to him now that he would be unable to pay his fare? He would not even hesitate to kill him.

The man decided to continue in good spirits as though nothing unusual had happened. It was common for the captain to spend a few hours with him each day. On this particular day, the captain said to him: "I know that you are smart and honest. I wish to purchase wheat to sell in London. However, I am afraid that I may be accused of stealing from the King's treasury. Therefore, let this purchase be under your name, and I will pay you well." The man agreed.

Upon arriving in London, the captain died suddenly and all his wheat remained with the man. This turned out to be much more than the original diamond was really worth.

The Rebbe completed this story by saying that the diamond did not belong to the man; as proof, it did not remain with him. The wheat was meant to be his; as proof, it did remain with him. And the reason he came upon his good fortune was because he controlled himself in his misfortune.

Kapcin Pascha

Once there was a Jew who was much favored by the king of Turkey. The king was more fond of this Jew than of all of his royal ministers. Each day the king would invite the Jew to his Palace to delight with him, as the royal ministers looked on jealously. They tried to find ways to libel him so that he would lose his favor with the king.

Among the ministers was one called Kapcin Pascha who detested this Jew more than everyone else did, but did not show these feelings openly. He too, tried to find a way to cause the downfall of the Jew.

One day, this Pascha came to the Jew and maliciously told him that he had just been to see the king and the king had confided in him of how fond he was of the Jew. However, the king finds one thing quite unbearable — that when the Jew speaks there is a foul odor emanating from his mouth. He cannot bear to be without him, yet he suffers so much in his presence. The Pascha advised the Jew that each time he appears before the King he should hold a handkerchief soaked in perfume near his mouth. The perfume would overcome the foul odor. The Jew, in his innocence, believed the Pascha and intended to do as the Pascha suggested.

The Pascha then went to the king and told him that he had just been to see the Jew, who declared to him that he suffers very much from the foul odor which emanates from the king's mouth, and finds it very difficult to speak with the king. He therefore suggests that the king clutch a sweet-smelling handkerchief near his mouth to make himself pleasant to speak to. To prove to the king that these words are true, the sign will be that when the Jew comes to the king, he himself will be holding a sweet-smelling handkerchief near his own mouth.

The king became very agitated when he heard this and said that when the Pascha's words are proven true he shall have revenge the life of the Jew. And so, the Jew came to the king as usual the very next day, and sure enough he was clutching a sweet-smelling handkerchief near his mouth as the Pascha had bade him to do. when the king saw that the Pascha was correct, he immediately wrote a letter saying these words: "The bearer of this letter must be thrust into the burning furnace; he deserves to die." The king placed his royal stamp on the note and asked to Jew to please deliver the note to a specific address. The Jew promised the King he would do so, not knowing the contents of the letter.

It happened that this Jew was accustomed to circumcise Jewish children. When requested to do so, he would immediately turn to this most important mitzvah. This very day he was asked to perform a circumcision (because Hashem wished to save him). He had to go without delay and circumcise the baby.

And what of the letter that the king had asked him to deliver? Hashem caused the Pascha to cross the Jew's path just then, and the Jew confided his dilemma to him. Would he deliver the letter instead? Of course, the Pascha was very happy to do so, because it provided him with yet another opportunity to inform the king about the Jew. The Pascha took the letter and delivered it to the person appointed for the special task, who seized the Pascha and threw him into the burning furnace, which he deserved according to the judgment of Hashem.

The Jew knew nothing of this and the next day he came before the king as usual. The king was truly perplexed and asked him if he had not yet delivered the letter. The Jew replied that the letter had reached its destination through the Kapcin Pascha because he himself had been in a hurry to perform a mitzvah of circumcision which had come his way by the will of Hashem. It was his custom never to delay in this great mitzvah. Only then did the king realize that the Pascha had maliciously informed on the Jew. The king asked the Jew, why did he hold a sweet-smelling handkerchief to his mouth in his presence? He replied that this was the advice of the Pascha, because the king could not bear the odor of his mouth. The king then related to the Jew all that the Pascha had done and also what he had written in the letter. The king declared that now he saw that Hashem rules the world and rescues his people from all bad. The Pascha received the very punishment he wanted inflicted upon the Jew. From that day on, the Jew's favor grew to greater heights in the eyes of the king.

Story about Maror (bitter herbs)

Once there were a Jew and a German wandering together. The Jew had taught the German to pose as a Jew. (The German language and the Jewish one are similar). This way the benevolent Jews will pity him.

Because it was the Eve of Passover, he taught the German how to behave at a Seder (as he would surely be invited to one by a Jew). He related to him the sequence of the entire Seder, except that he forgot to tell him about the Maror.

The German came to the Passover Seder very hungry from not eating all day, and looked forward to partaking of all the good foods his Jewish friend had told him about. However, he was first given a piece of Karpas dipped into salt water, and the other things customarily eaten, and then the Hagadah was recited, with the stories describing at length the exodus of the Jewish people from Egypt with all of the commentaries. He was waiting impatiently for the meal and was indeed happy to see that the Matzo was finally being eaten. Suddenly he was given some Maror and his mouth became bitter. Thinking that this was what the entire meal consisted of, he fled, thinking: "Cursed Jews, after all that ceremony, this is all they eat?" He went to the Beth Medrash and slept. The Jew arrived happily shortly together, having fully satisfied his hunger, and asked the German how it went with him. The German angrily related the events of the evening until his flight. How silly of him, replied the Jew; had he been patient only a while longer he would have eaten to his heart's content!

After exerting much effort and finally coming closer to the ways of Hashem in purifying the body, one tastes some bitterness and retreats, thinking that bitterness is all he will sense. However, one who is patient and waits a while longer, bearing the bitterness, will be rewarded with revitalization and joy. (One may obtain lessons from these analogies in all types of serving G-d.) One may at first find it bitter and difficult, but later he reaps enjoyment.

The Treasure Under the Bridge:

Once, a man dreamt that under a certain bridge in Vienna lay buried treasure. He traveled to Vienna and came to the bridge and stood there wondering how to obtain the treasure.

During the day he could not do anything, because there were many people about. Another man passed by and asked him what he was up to. The first man decided to reveal the dream to him so he could help him and then they would share the treasure. The man replied: "I have also dreamt of a treasure hidden in the home of this and this man residing in such and such country, (actually the very person he was speaking to). Should I travel to him?" Hearing this, the first man realized the treasure was in his own home. He returned home and searched and found the hidden treasure. "Now I know, the treausre was always in my possession, but to become aware of it I had to travel to Vienna."

This is how it is with serving G-d — the treasure is within each person, but in order to discover it one must travel to a Righteous Person.

The Story of the Turkey:

Once there was the son of a king, who had lost his mind thinking he was a turkey. He would sit naked under a table and eat the crumbs and bones off the floor. All the doctors lost hope in curing him of this malady and the king was very sad.

Finally, a person came and said that he would cure him. This wise man removed his clothing and joined the king's son under the table. "Who are you" asked the son, "and what are you doing here?" "Who are you," said the wise man, "and what are *you* doing here?" "I am a turkey," said the son. "I am also a turkey," said the wise man. So they both sat there together for some time until they grew accustomed to each other.

Then the wise man signaled, and shirts were given to him. The wise man said, "Do you think that a turkey cannot wear a shirt? One can wear a shirt and still be a turkey." So they both put on a shirt.

After a while, he signaled and some pants were given to him. He told the son, did he think that if he wore pants he would not be a turkey anymore? One could wear pants and still be a turkey. Soon they both put on the pants, and so on.

Then he signaled and humans' food was given to him and he said to the king's son: "Do you think that if one eats humans' food one cannot remain a turkey? We can eat and still be turkeys." Then he said: "One can be a turkey and eat while sitting at a table." He finally cured the king's son completely.

The moral here is self-explanatory. Should one say that one who wants to become close to G-d cannot do so for he is like a turkey, in the sense that he is human and materialistic? That is not so; step by step one can come closer and closer to serving G-d until he succeeds.

Parable about Wheat:

One time a king told his assistant, "The stars foretold about the wheat that they will grow this year, that all who eat it will lose their minds. Let us therefore find some solution." The assistant said, "We can prepare wheat from another world source for our own consumption."

"If so," said the king, "The whole world will be crazy and we will be the only two normal people. It would seem as though we were the ones who are crazy. It would be impossible to prepare enough wheat for the whole world so we might as well eat that wheat also, but we will make a sign on each other's foreheads. When we will look at each other we will be reminded by the sign that we are actually crazy.

HIS TALES

The Prince who was made of Precious Stones

There was once a king who had no children. He spent much time and energy consulting with doctors and specialists for he feared greatly that his kingdom would be inherited by strangers. The doctors were unable to help him. Then he decreed that the Jews should pray that he be blessed with children. The Jews went looking for a Righteous Man whose prayer would be answered so that there would be children. They searched until they found an unknown Tzadik, A Righteous Person, and they told him to pray for the king to have sons. He answered that he didn't know anything. So they went and told the king, and the king sent his Sergeant at Arms after him. He brought the Tzadik to the king. The king tried to convince him, using the "positive" approach. He said, "You know, all the Jews here are in my hands, for me to do with them as I wish. With that in mind, I ask you nicely, pray for me that I may have sons.". The Tzadik then promised him that within a year he would have a child.

The Tzadik returned to his place, and within the year, the Queen gave birth to a daughter. This Princess was unusually beautiful. When she was four years old she was educated, and she knew how to play musical instruments. She was also good at languages. Kings came from all different countries just to see her, and the king was very happy. But after awhile, he became obsessed with the idea that he must have a son. He still worried that, although he had a daughter, his kingdom might fall into strange hands through marriage.

And so, once again he decreed that the Jews must pray for him to have a son. The Jews went searching for that same Tzadik, but they couldn't find him because he had already passed away from this world. Still, they kept on looking until they found another hidden Tzadik. And they told him, "Give the king a son." He said he knew nothing, and they so informed the king.

The king had him brought to Court as he did in the previous case, and he spoke to him as he had to the other Tzadik, saying, "The Jews are in my hands," etc. The Tzadik asked the king, "Can you do what I ask of you?" The king said yes. The Tzadik said, "It is necessary that you gather all kinds of jewels and gems, for each jewel has its own special charm. Kings have a book listing all the different types of jewels." The king said, "I would give half my kingdom for a son," and he went and brought back all kinds of precious stones and jewels. The Tzadik took them and crushed them, and then mixed them into a solution of wine. He gave half a cup of this wine to the king, and half the cup to the queen, and they drank of this mixture. Then he said to them, "You will have a son who will be made of gems, and will in his essence be a collection of all the charms and qualities intrinsic in these many gems that you have supplied." And he returned to his home.

The queen gave birth to a son, and the king was exceedingly happy, even though the child was not made of gems. When he was four years old he was very handsome, and already knowledgeable, and spoke many languages. Kings now came to see him, and the princess was no longer the center of attraction. She became jealous of him. Her one consolation was that he was not made of jewels, as the Tzadik had predicted. Then one time, the prince was chopping wood and cut his finger. When the princess ran over to bandage him she saw a gem on the cut. She was overcome with jealousy and pretended to be sick.

Doctors were summoned from all over, but they were unable to cure her mysterious illness. So magicians were summoned. One of these magicians realized what was the matter, and revealed to her that he knew she was only pretending to be ill. Seeing that he knew his profession well, she asked him if he could perform such witchcraft as would cause a person to become ill with leprosy. The magician said he could do that. The princess pursued the subject: What if another magician was called to cure this same person? Would he get well? The magician explained that if the disease was caused by way of an evil talisman, and after it had done its work it was thrown into the sea, no one could undo the magic.

Following his instructions, she carried out the bewitchment, and then threw the talisman into the ocean. The prince became leprous. The leprosy attacked his nose, his face, and the rest of his body. The king sent for all the best doctors, and then for magicians, but none of them were able to help in this matter. Finally, he decreed that the Jews pray. The Jews searched out the Tzadik who had helped on the previous occaseion, and brought him to the king. Now this Tzadik was always praying to G-d regarding the fact that he had promised that the child would be made of gems and this did not occur. He complained to the Al-mighty, "Was it for my honor that I promised this? No, I have done nothing but for the sake of your honor! And now it is an embarrassment that I promised something and it didn't happen."

He was taken to the king. He prayed for the health of the prince, but his prayers did not help. Then he was informed (from above) that this was a witchcraft. He went to the king and informed him that an evil talisman had been used and that it had then been thrown into the ocean; so there was no chance to help the prince unless the person who had bewitched him was himself thrown into the ocean. The king said, "I'll give you all the magicians of my kingdom. Throw them into the sea if this will help my son." The princess heard this and was frightened. She ran to the water to recover the talisman, for she knew where it lay. But when she came near, she fell into the water. This caused a big commotion. Everyone was worried and excited by the fact that the princess had fallen! While this was going on, the Tzadik approached the king once again, and said, "Fear not, the prince will become well."

In fact the prince recovered. The leprosy that had afflicted him began to dry, and his skin began to peel off. And lo and behold, under his skin he was revealed to be made entirely of jewels. And all that knew him realized that he had the charms and qualities of those many gems.

The Spider and the Fly

There was once a king who had many difficult wars. He won them all and took many captives. (After the Rabbi had already begun this story he interrupted himself, saying, "Do you think that if I tell everything, you will understand?)". The king made a big banquet each year on the anniversary of his victory. All the ministers were invited and there was entertainment, especially comedy. The comedians' special attraction was a farce that they performed, in which they parodied the customs of the different peoples. They parodied all the nations of the world, the Arabs and others; and they made fun of Jews too. The king ordered that he be brought a book in which was recorded the customs of each and every nation. He opened the book at different places, and saw that wherever he looked, the customs of each nation were recorded much as they had been parodied by the comedians. Apparently, the comedians had seen this same book.

As he sat there, looking at the book, he noticed a spider moving across the edges of the pages that were on one side of this open book. And at the opposite end of the book there was a fly. And where would the spider go, if not toward the fly? But there was a breeze that lifted a page of the book. And this page was like a partition that stood between the spider and the fly, preventing the spider from approaching the fly. The spider started moving back toward the edge of the book as if she'd lost interest in the fly. The page fell back to its original position. Once again, the spider started across the open book, but then the page lifted as it had before, not letting the spider get across. This happened a number of times. After a while the spider grew bold. She was part of the way across when the page lifted as before, but this time came down on the other side of the center, trapping the spider, who was then caught between two pages. The spider scratched a bit till she sank down and was lost. (And I won't tell you what happened to the fly)

The king watched all this with great wonder, for he realized there was some meaning in what he had seen. All the ministers watched the king staring at the book and they wondered too. The king started thinking about what he had seen and what it could mean, and he dozed as he sat there with the book.

He had a dream. In his dream he held in his hand a gem, a diamond. He looked at it, and there appeared to be caricatures of people coming out of it. He threw the gem down. Now, it is the practice of kings to have this portrait made. On the head of the portrait they place the crown when it is not actually worn. And these people who came out of the diamond took the portrait and cut off its head, and took the crown and threw it into the mud. Then, in the dream, he saw these people coming after him to kill him. But a page of the book he was lying upon rose and defended him. With this page protecting him, they could do him no evil, and they left him. After that, when the page fell back to its place, they ran at him again to kill him, and the page rose again as before. This was repeated a number of times.

He had a great desire to know which page was defending him. Which nation's customs were inscribed on that page? Yet he feared to look. He started to yell, "What a shame, what a shame." All the ministers who were sitting around heard his cries. They wanted to wake him, but it is not respectful to wake a king. Then, as he continued to dream, a great mountain came to him. The mountain said, "Why were you yelling? For a long time now, I have been asleep, and nothing could wake me, but you woke me." So he answered, "How could I not scream with them coming to kill me?· It is only this page that protected me." The mountain replied; "If that is the page that defends you, you have nothing to fear. For I, too, have many enemies who attack me, and this page is my sole defense. Come, I'll show you." And he showed him that around the mountain there were thousands and tens of thousand of enemies who were feasting and celebrating, playing muscial instruments, and singing and dancing. What were they celebrating? When one of them, in one of the groups around the mountain thinks of a plan to get to the top, they all start celebrating and singing and eating, etc. This happens in each and every group. "And it is only this page of customs," said the mountain, "Which was your defense, that defends me too."

At the top of the mountain there was a tablet. The tablet showed which people's customs were written on the page that defended the mountain, but because the mountain was so high, no one could read what was written. At the foot of the mountain there was another sign. There it was written that only those who had all there teeth could ascend the mountain. But the Al-mighty allowed grass to grow at the foot of the mountain, where one had to pass in order to ascend. People would lose their teeth as soon as they came upon the grass. It made no difference if they came on foot or in a vehicle; whether they rode in a carriage or rode on animals. As soon as they came to the grass their teeth would fall out. There were great piles of teeth there, hills and hills of teeth.

Then these same people that the king had seen earlier came back and put his portrait back together. They lifted the crown out of the mud and washed it. They put the crown back on the portrait, and the king woke up.

The king immediately looked at the page that had defended him, to see which nation's customs were described on that page. The customs that he found there were those of the people of Israel. He studied the page and he saw truth there. It was an inspiration for him that here was the Truth. He resolved that he would surely become a Jew. But what couwd he do to influence the rest of the people in this direction? How could he bring them to the truth? He decided to go looking for a Wise Man, one who could interpret the dream he had dreamt. He took two men with him, and went out into the world to search for such a Wise Man. He didn't travel as a king, but disguised himself as a simple man. Traveling from town to town, and from country to country, he inquired as to the whereabouts of a Wise Man who could interpret dreams and explain their contents. Eventually he heard of such a man in a certain place, and he went there and found him. To this man he told the truth. He told him that he was a king; he told him about his victories at war, and all that has already been related in this story. Then he asked him to interpret his dream.

The Wise Man told him: "I myself can't interpret your dream. But what I can do is that at the proper time, on the right day, on the right month, I will gather together certain herbs, and make an incense mixture of them. And one who smokes this incense mixture will be able to think his thoughts, and what he wants to know he will know." The king waited. Though it had already taken his time to find this man, he waited until the right time for the man to prepare the mixture as he said he would. Finally the time came, the herbs were prepared, and he smoked the incense.

After he had smoked the mixture he began to see things that had happened even before his own birth, when he was still just a soul in the World Above. He saw how his soul was led through the Above Worlds. Then it was announced: IF ANYONE HAS A COMPLAINT AGAINST THIS SOUL, LET HIM COME FORWARD. No one complained. Suddenly someone came running. He shouted, "Master of the Universe, if this soul comes to the world, what will be left for me? What did you create me for?" The person that was shouting was the Satan himself. He was answered: "This soul must certainly go down to the world. You will think of some plan." The Satan then went on his way. The soul was led through the passages of the Above World until he came to the Heavenly Court, to be sworn to serve G-d. When he was ready to be sent down, the complainant still had not appeared, so a messenger was sent to bring him. The messenger returned with the Satan, who had with him an old man who was bent the way old men are, yet was quite familiar. He laughed, and said, "I have found a plan. You can send him down now." Then the soul was awlowed to enter the world. The king saw all that had happened to him from the beginning to the end; how he was made king, the wars he fought, etc.

The Rabbi and his Only Son

There was a Rabbi who was childless for some time until he was blessed with a son. He raised him lovingly, and when the young man was old enough, found him a proper bride. The son was given an upstairs room so he could continue his studies undisturbed, as was the custom of the well-to-do in that area. The son was conscientious. He spent his time in study and prayer. But he had the feeling that there was something missing in his life. Sometimes he didn't feel complete devotion when he prayed, or it seemed as if he missed the inner reason in his study. He spoke of this lack to two of his young comrades, and they suggested that he visit a certain Righteous Man, a Tzadik. This young man had already reached the level where he'd become a *small light* in the world, by virtue of his good deeds.

The young man went and told his father about his feelings, that there was a certain tastelessness in his religious life, and that this lack bothered him. He didn't know what caused it, and wished to go and consult with this certain Tzadik about whom he'd heard. His father did his best to discourage the son regarding this plan. He asked, "Why go to him? You yourself are a greater scholar than he is. And you come from a better family. It doesn't seem right for you to go to one such as he. Forget about it." The father continued in this manner till he succeeded in preventing the trip. And the son returned to his studies.

Some time later he was once again disturbed by this same problem, and again he consulted with his friends about the lack that he felt. As before, they suggested that he travel to see the Tzadik. He told his father that he wished to go. His father tried to divert him, and persuaded and argued as before until he succeeded in preventing the trip. This occurred again and again, a number of times.

Each time he would feel an internal emptiness that he longed to fill, yet he was not certain what was troubling him. Finally he went to his father and pleaded with him till his father could no longer refuse. Yet, because this was his only son, the Rabbi did not want him to take the trip alone and decided to accompany him. To his son, he said, "All right, you may go, and I'll go with you. But you'll eventually see that he wasn't worth the trip."

They traveled by coach. Along the way, the father said: 'If all goes well on this trip, we'll know it was meant to be. But if we start encountering troubles along the way, let us take that as a sign from Heaven that we weren't meant to go. In that case, we'll return home." Eventually they came to a bridge and the horse stumbled. The carriage was overturned, and they were nearly drowned. His father said, "You can see that this trip wasn't meant to be," and they turned around and went back. The son returned to his studies. But once again he felt this lack that he couldn't identify, and again he pleaded with his father until he obtained his father's consent, and they traveled together as before.

This time, as before, his father made it a condition that they would continue on this venture only as long as all went well, and that they would interpret difficulties along the way as a sign from Heaven that they were not to make this trip. As they were traveling, both the axles of the carriage broke. The Rabbi said, "This is a sure sign that we weren't meant to take this trip. It is unnatural for both axles to break. Many times we have traveled in this coach, yet these things never happened." So they returned, and the young man went back to his holy ways. But the same problem revisited him. Again he became dejected by these feelings, and again he spoke to his friends of this matter. Their advice, as before, was that he really should go to see this Tzadik. And he explained his great desire to his father, and his father gave in, and agreed to go. But this time the son said to his father, "Let's not interpret what happens along the way as signs from Heaven. It is only natural that a horse will stumble now and then, or that an axle will break. Unless we encounter something really unusual that can't be ignored, let us complete this trip."

They traveled along the way, and when they got to an inn, they stopped for the night. There they met a businessman. They got into the sort of typical conversation that one has on the road, with casual encounters. They didn't mention where they were going because the Rabbi was a little embarrassed by the whole affair, and by the fact that they were going such a distance just to visit a Righteous Man. They spoke of politics, and the affairs of the world. Without discussing things in depth, they moved from subject to subject till they found themselves talking about tzadikim, and where Righteous People were to be found. The businessman mentioned a Tzadik that he had heard of in a certain place, and then spoke of another one in another place, and still another one that people sometimes went to visit, or to ask for his blessing. And so they mentioned the name of the Tzadik (that they were going to visit). To which, the businessman remarked, "*Him? He's nothing!* I just happen to be coming back from a visit with him myself, and I observed him in the act of a transgression!" The father then spoke to the young man, "You see, my son, what this man says in a passing manner, and he's coming from there." So they turned around and went home.

Soon thereafter, the son died. After he had died he appeared in a dream to the Rabbi, his father. The Rabbi saw him standing before him, very angry. He asked, "What is this anger?" The son replied that he should go to this same Tzadik that the son had always wanted to visit, and he would explain to the father why the son was

angry. The father woke up and dismissed what he had
seen, as "just a dream." Then, some time later, he had the
same dream again. He did not take it seriously, thinking
that it was just because of his sadness at having lost his
son. But when he had had this same dream three times, he
was impressed. He set out to visit the Tzadik. On his way
he met the same businessman that he had met on the
previous trip, when he had been traveling with his son.
He recognized him, and said, "Didn't we once meet in an
inn?

The man said: "We certainly did!" And the Rabbi was
surprised by the tone of his voice, and even more so by
what the man said next, "If you want, I could swallow
you!" "What are you saying?" asked the Rabbi.

"Do you remember," said the man, "how you traveled
with your son, and the first time the horse fell off the
bridge and you returned? The next time the axles broke.
And after that you met me. And I told you that the Tzadik
was nothing special? Well now that I've gotten rid of your
son, you can go on with your visit. Your son was the
Small Light in this world, and the Tzadik is the *Great
Light*, and if the two of them had gotten together, the
Messiah would have come. But now that I've gotten rid of
him, you can go on alone." And while he was speaking, he
suddenly disappeared. The shocked Rabbi found himself
standing alone.

The Rabbi then continued on his way to the Tzadik.
And he shouted, "Oh what a shame, oh what a shame for
that which is lost and cannot be forgotten. May the
blessed Lord bring back the dispersed very soon, Amen."

(The businessman was the Satan himself, that fooled
them. Later, when he met the Rabbi, he berated him for
following his advice, for that is his custom.) May G-d
save us from him.

Gevald!!! Never give up hope.

It is forbidden for one to give up hope.

It is a very great Mitzvoh for one to be constantly happy.

Meditation is a very high level. In fact it is above all other levels.

If you believe that you can spoil, believe that you can correct.

Know, that a person walks in life on a very narrow bridge. The most important rule is not to be afraid.

Even when things appear to be at their worst, it can instantly turn around for the persons full benefit.

A person for the pleasure of a quarter of an hour can lose his portion in this world as well as in the After-world.

When asked, "What is in reality the power of choice?" the Rebbe answered "Simple. If you want, you do, if not, not. Too many people are trapped in the customs of their habits, but if they truly want to, they can easily overcome."

Although the Land of Israel appears to be as ordinary as any other land nevertheless, it is very great and awesome in its holiness. The same is true of a righteous man, He appears as others do, yet his inner being is completely holy and different from the average man.

Said Rabbi Nachman: "Everyone says there is a present life and an After-world." Concerning the afterworld, we believe there is one. As of the present world possibly it exists somewhere. Here however, seeing what suffering crosses everyones path, it appears that this is the Gehnnom.

Drunkedness causes a person to forget the will of G-d.

A person must be very stubborn when it comes to the serving of G-d.

No one is ever given an obstacle that he cannot overcome.

The thoughts of a person are like a horse with reins. They can be controlled with a simple shifting of the mind.

The truth is only one. A silver cup can be only silver. To call it anything else but exactly what it is, is an untruth.

The desire to triumph cannot endure the truth. Even were the individual shown clearly his error, he would not concede.

There are people who appear to be praying, studying and fulfilling their religious objectives, and yet they are in truth sleeping away their years. A person must inject life and feeling into his day.

One cannot rise to great spiritual heights without the holiness of the Land of Israel.

Every Jew has a portion in the Holy Land.

Arrogance and adultery are bound together.

A person's clothes shall always be whole and neat.

Arrogance is akin to idolatry.

Give charity before you set out on a journey.

That man is distant from serving G-d, is due to his lack of meditation. True meditation is achieved only through joy.

To be steeped in the desire for money is likened to idol worship.

The desire for money can warp a persons mind from facing reality.

True faith can be achieved only by attaining a solid faith in the Tzaddikim.

One must always look for the good points in every single Jew.

Peace comes when there is truth.

Peace is the sign of life.

From the moment that a person considers repentance, his prayers are accepted.

The serving of G-d in the young years (when the Evil One is at his strongest) even one day is worth more than a few years of an elderly man.

Even though a person falls from his serving G-d, those few days that one sacrificed for G-d remain very precious in His eyes.

Sur meyra va'ase tov (psalms 34) "Leave evil and do good". Occupy yourself with doing good deeds and the bad will automatically fall away.

There are times when Hashem will aid a person in this world and he can feel the pleasures of the After-world.

Concerning wars that take place between nations, Rabbi

Nachman remarked, "see how wise and intelligent these people are, constantly thinking and planning to invent the ultimate weapon that can in one moment wipe out thousands upon thousands of people.

Faith may be on the lowest level, but only through faith one can attain the highest of all levels.

The main mitzvah that is entitled "doing" is the act of charity.

A student was once complaining to Rabbi Nachman about his lack of accomplishment in serving G-d. He said that he wanted very much to serve G-d. Rabbi Nachman said to him "Do you *truly want* to desire?"

ON BRESLOV

There seems to be considerable confusion among English writers about how to spell Rabbi Nachman's city.

We have chosen to use the spelling Breslov, which is preferred by all English speaking followers of Rabbi Nachman. It is the spelling used on the stationery of the Breslover Yeshiva in Jerusalem, as well as a number of synagogues founded by his followers.

There is considerable evidence from oral tradition that this was the way the name was pronounced in the time of Rabbi Nachman. This is supported by the *Shivechay HaBaal Shem Tov,* published in 1815. Here we find the town spelled and vocalized as Breslov (Jerusalem, 5729, p. 60. This is based on the 1815 Berdichov edition).

In Rabbi Nathan's work such as *Sichos HaRan, Chayay Moharan,* and *Alim LeTerufah,* we find it spelled BRSLV, without vocalization. It is not until the late nineteenth century that we find it vocalized Brasliv (*Tovos Zichronos,* p. 7).

Bratzlav, the spelling adapted by most contemporary writers, is based on a transliteration of the modern Russian.

Other variant spellings are Brazlaw (Steiler's Handatlas), Braclav (Rand McNally, McGraw Hill), Bratslav (Pergamon, Times) and Braslavl (Jewish Encyclopedia).

Situated on the right bank of the River Bug, midway between Nemerov and Tulchin in the government of Podolia (48° 49′ N., 28° 53′ E.) Breslov had a Jewish population of 2500 out of a general population of six thousand.

A historic Jewish community, it was the scene of major Jewish massacres in 1479, 1551, 1561, 1648 and 1664. For a while it was the home of Rabbi Naftali Katz, and ancestor of Rabbi Nachman who embarked on a similar journey to the Holy Land. The town also figured in a number of episodes involing the Baal Shem Tov.

Rabbi Nachman once said that BReSLoV has the same letters as *LeV BaSaR* — the "heart of flesh" that the prophet Ezekiel (11:19) said that every Jew must have. He said that his followers would always be known as Breslover Chasidim.

ספר קדוש זה הודפס ומוקדש לזכר נשמת

האי גברא רבא ויקירא

גריס באורייתא תדירא

מרבה חכמה יוסיף דעת

גדל החסד כביר המעש

רב הפעלים נודע בשערים

האציל מרוחו לקרובים ולרחוקים

גדר פרץ ועמד בשער

הקים עולה של תורה בכל אתר

הרב צבי ארי׳ בן-ציון ב״ר ישראל אבא רוזנפלד ז״ל

נשיא ישיבת "חסידי ברסלב" אור הנעלם

בעיה״ק ירושלים ת״ו

נפטר בקרתא קדישא ירושלם

ונטמן בהר הזיתים המקודש

י״א כסלו תשל״ט